The Barefoot Helper

Mindfulness and Creativity
in Social Work and the
Caring Professions

Mark Hamer

D1328590

Russell House Publishing

Russell House Publishing
First published in 2006 by:
Russell House Publishing Ltd.
4 St. George's House
Uplyme Road
Lyme Regis
Dorset DT7 3LS
Tel: 01297-443948
Fax: 01297-442722
e-mail: help@russellhouse.co.uk
www.russellhouse.co.uk

British Library Cataloguing-in-publication Data:

A catalogue record for this book is available from the British Library.

ISBN: 978-1-905541-03-4

Typeset by TW Typesetting, Plymouth, Devon
Printed by Biddles Ltd, King's Lynn

Contents

For Daisy and Oscar, my children,
who have taught me more than they will ever know.
As I grow older, I begin to understand that the
child really is the father of the man.

Acknowledgements

Writing this little book has been like going into a fantastic grotto filled with jewels, gold and precious artefacts. I felt like Aladdin as I plundered and rummaged and carried away as much as my bulging pockets hold. There are many beautiful and inspiring ideas out there in the world. Ideas which explore humanity, which express the beauty and poetry of life. I have taken the words and ideas which caught my eye and which fitted in with what I wanted to say. I hope I have credited everybody whose words I have recycled.

This is a little book, it can only hold so much and I have had to be ruthless in my editing. There is much I would have liked to say, both in feeling and content. But I am confident that if I strike a chord with the reader, if I plant or nurture a seed, they will go much further with their exploration than I have been able to here.

I am eternally grateful to Geoffrey Mann at Russell House for his invaluable support and encouragement through the tough times which are part of the process of writing a book, and for his tireless efforts in helping me to knock it into a publishable shape from my stream of consciousness ramblings. I am also grateful to Martin Calder who, although he may not be aware of it, has encouraged me very much in my writing, also to the readers who have taken the trouble to send me their thoughts about my other work.

About the Author

I am a practising social worker and therapist in the Option 2 Project in Cardiff. This is an award winning service that works with families in crisis. When childcare professionals are about to remove children from their families we become involved and help families to make real changes so they can remain together as families. We have trained practitioners from across the UK in our solution-focussed model and they are reporting some very positive outcomes. We concern ourselves with outcomes for families rather than input and so our trusting management style has created a place where real social work is valued. We use a model that has spectacular outcomes for families at the hard end of the child protection system. You can read more about it on my website www.another-way.co.uk and in my previous book *Preventing Breakdown* which is available from the same publisher.

This is a very different kind of book, a much more personal one. I hope you enjoy reading it and I would be delighted if you got in touch with me. No, really, I would enjoy hearing from you with your thoughts and comments. Writing is a lonely business and I still get excited when I get emails! John Stuart Mill said that every movement must experience three stages: ridicule, discussion and adoption and I expect responses to this book that will fit into each of Mills' categories, so please don't hold back! I like to think of this as an open source model, if you feel you can improve it, teach me how, and if I am lucky enough for this book to reach a second edition then I may be able to incorporate your ideas.

Who This Book is Aimed at

If you work with people – sick people, hurting, abused or abusing people, violent people, people without hope, failing people, drug misusing, drinking, worried or frightened people, the ideas in this book may help you. I believe they can help you to do your job better and can help you to stay sane and happy in a challenging role. I have written it mainly with social workers in mind because that is a world I know and understand. Yet this is a book primarily about working with people in distress and how you can do that in the most enabling way for them and for you. So if your role, in whatever setting, is to help people who are going through difficult times, if your role is to help people to change their lives, then this book is for you.

'Mark Hamer has a rare facility for planting the seeds of positive change and genuinely help people to use their own creativity to break out of harmful behaviour patterns. His book is written for anyone whose work is devoted to alleviating human suffering. It provides the self-empowering tools and philosophy to do so effectively and remain sane. Mark's love shines out through every word – the book's filled with compassion and joy and yet is immensely practical. If you work in the caring professions you could do far worse than to spend a few hours reading this. Doing so could change your life and by extension, the lives of everyone you touch, for the better. I endorse it wholeheartedly.'

The Guardian's Barefoot Doctor

Introduction

Social work is a profession I care about, something I enjoy doing and that is valid in our world, but sometimes it is not all it could be. I think it can feel better for clients and better for workers more often than it does. I believe you can be happy as a social worker, loved by clients and colleagues, and a damn good social worker with a good reputation and good career prospects. Furthermore, I also believe you can be effective and professional and yet shrug off the dulling constraints of corporate uniformity and be your own unique, individual self. In fact I believe you have to access your own personal creativity in order to do good social work. There is a way of doing social work that celebrates the human spirit and embraces the creativity that defines human beings, a way that encourages clients to get to know who they really are and what they really want, a way that helps them to create clear goals based on their insights. I know that there is a way of working that will help you to feel good about what you do more often.

You may have already guessed that this is not your usual social work book. I don't talk here about published guidance, or messages from research. I will not be quoting any statistics, but there is a list of resources at the end of the book so readers can follow any particular threads they find appealing. This is a book about ideas and putting them into practice. They are ideas that I hope you will find useful, practical, thought-provoking and supportive.

Where are we heading?

Over the years I have seen social work practice become more bureaucratic, less humane and less connected to the daily lives of the people who use our services. Many social workers have become case managers, practicing by telephone and computer, tied up with client record systems and care plans, arranging other services to visit their clients for them. In one area I am familiar with social workers, once based in the community, now work from an out of town call centre which provides the public with no access to their social worker. Nearly 100 workers practice on each of three floors. The workers themselves have no personal space, no sound barriers between them, there is no space for quiet reflection, no facility to make a quiet telephone call with a grieving client. They have no personal control over temperature, ventilation and noise levels, no doors to close, even no walls to put up pictures. When pictures are put up on the posh wooden filing cabinets they are removed by workers in the night. Environments like these are purposely designed to stifle creativity and create people who are easily managed, easily observed and will do as they are told. In such an environment, creativity feels threatening. When workers voice their rebellion, their words are wasted. Complaints are met with blank indifference.

Sometimes the systems we work within can breed a sense of hopelessness, taking excitement and creativity away from workers. If our role is to help people to be free of the shackles of destructive behaviour patterns, self-defeating thought processes, poor skills in parenting, self-care, relationships and communication and if we are to help people to create new lives, then we as workers need to feel creative, need to feel free to do work that is personal and individual to the clients unique needs.

Changing your life is a creative process that comes from the imagination and so clients need to be able to be creative. If our own creativity is stifled, then it becomes difficult to foster the creativity in others that encourages them to pursue the kinds of lives they hope to have. If, however, our role is to monitor, to control, to measure, to oppress, then we are well on the way to achieving that aim.

A quiet shift in values

Around me, in my daily life, I can see a quiet shift in personal values. Individuals around me are thinking about how we choose to make a living, what we choose to eat, how we spend our free time, what we do with our leisure time, what we believe about life and our place in the world, how we make ourselves fit and healthy and how we look after our planet.

The Slow Food movement in Italy, based on cooking real food at home for family and friends, has expanded to become the Slow City movement, where traffic is reduced and fast food outlets are restricted. My own employers are making efforts to concern themselves with the work/life balance of their employees, conscious that happy people are productive people. They are bringing masseurs into the workplace, promoting lunchtime walks and running yoga classes.

Many people are becoming concerned about pollutants in our atmosphere, their CO_2 footprint and the freshness of the food they eat. They are changing their diets to exclude foods treated with chemicals, genetically engineered or that have travelled long and polluting distances. We are focussing on the ethics of what we choose to eat. City dwellers are buying fresh, organic and locally produced food from farmer's markets which come to town, on Sundays, supporting local growers, developing local communities and traders and helping individuals to live a life that does the least harm. People are making changes and trying to create lives which are more ethical, more balanced between work and play, love and life, lives which are physically, spiritually and emotionally healthy for themselves and others. All of these actions, this sense of mindfulness, spring from beliefs about individual responsibility and love.

This is a grass roots movement in which people are transforming society not by political or social action, but by quietly making choices about their own lives, thinking about their beliefs and activities and changing them for the better. It is a movement of individual souls, with no leader, no clear organisation or structure and practically invisible, yet when you start to look you will find evidence for it. A Sunday magazine has a regular barefoot columnist; a clothing company in West Wales has an article in its catalogue about what makes a decent loaf of bread. My favourite website at the moment is Freecycle. Instead of taking unwanted furniture, bicycles, cardboard boxes etc. to the dump, or trying to sell them on Ebay, people offer them to other members of the community for free. This reduces landfill and transport; builds community links, declutters lives and at the same time provides free things to people who can make use of them.

Workers are looking for ways to integrate their values into their work, looking for meaning and joy in their occupations, downsizing, downshifting and focussing on the quality of life instead of the collection of money and the display of prestige. People are feeling the need to slow down and look after themselves, looking to holistic solutions to life's difficulties.

Like the eternal Yin Yang symbol, darkness carries the seed of light, and so out of the self-obsessed attitudes of the 'Me generation' inevitably comes the socially responsible 'We generation' of ethical traders and consumers. People who take the time and energy to question their place in this world, their work, their actions, how they spend their time on this planet and how they can comfortably share space with the variety of other human souls around them and value their often very different ways of expression.

Such questions produce people-oriented individuals who embrace their individual creativity and consider how it can be used to make the world a better place, who consider every action and thought and try to add something positive and create a better life for everybody. And so individuals are developing their personal creativity and generally thinking about how their individual presence in the world can do the least harm and generally be a force for good.

A synthesis of ideas

Over thousands of years, people have been just people, living their lives and trying to make the best of things. Over the years they have learned stuff about how to live. Some people have dedicated their studies to the problems of being people, we can still use some of the stuff they have learned. In the past those people would have been shamans, then mystics, philosophers and priests, psychiatrists, psychologists, social workers and counsellors. Many have learned truths about the human condition, and I make no apologies that I have drawn my inspiration for this book from a combination of sources; from Taoism, Yoga and Hindu philosophy, Christian mysticism and occult thought, Zen Buddhism and more recent thinking about brief solution-focussed therapy, cognitive behavioural therapy, motivational interviewing, neuro-linguistic programming and life coaching.

Time and time again in my reading, these often vastly different world views have hit me with the same themes, that happiness comes from:

- doing the least harm
- focused effort
- clarity of thought
- respect
- awareness

- clear goals

- taking time not just to act and do things, but also stopping doing things from time to time, and experiencing life directly.

This synthesis of ideas is the essence of barefoot philosophy.

How social workers can do the least harm

In this book I want to explore how helpers can do the least harm. This is a practice I aspire to as a social worker and a human being. I am concerned with how we treat ourselves, our colleagues, our clients and our environment. I believe that work should be liberating, meaningful and fulfilling for workers and clients. This is a creative approach that creates positive outcomes for workers, clients and even the systems we work within.

This thoughtfulness about living a life that does the least harm easily migrates into ideas about how human and professional relationships can do the least harm. How can we work as professionals with vulnerable clients and do the least harm to ourselves, to our colleagues, to the individuals we support? If workers are to create progress in the gentlest and most holistic way possible while doing the least harm, this philosophy needs to be embodied equally by managers and teams.

To do the least harm while promoting change, you have to be aware of where change occurs naturally, so that you can encourage and empower that change. This allows the client to grow in their own direction at their own pace. The social worker's role is to value, feed and nurture the client's growth. It allows you to experience the very life of spontaneous engagement with another human being, experience the full joy of living and being and doing good social work . . . no, more than that, this is a philosophy that will inspire you to do *fantastic* social work.

Social work as a positive force in the world

I also write this in a spirit of celebration, as a reminder that we are a positive force in the world, that we are creative human beings. It is a book about love in action, about joy and beauty, about caring, about the heart and soul of who we are and what we do. Having said that, I hope you find this an intensely practical and useful book that helps you think about how you do your thing.

If you go barefoot you tread lightly and carefully, living in and fully experiencing the moment. If you think of going barefoot as a metaphor for a way of living, then you will see that the idea quickly becomes very deep and considers issues such as sharing, communication and love. This is a holistic way of living and, as a social worker, it feels only right that I should use those beliefs in my work with clients. They want to feel whole too:

Going barefoot is the gentlest way of walking and can symbolise a way of living – being authentic, vulnerable, sensitive to our surroundings. It's the feeling of enjoying warm sand beneath our toes, or carefully making our way over sharp rocks in the darkness. It's a way of living that has the lightest impact, removing the barrier between us and nature.

Adele Coombs, *Barefoot Dreaming*

Chapter 1

Where we Are: The State of Social Work

I came into this profession to be a helper, and yet very early on in my career I began to feel that many of the very vulnerable people who I wanted to help were actually better off without me. 'On the job' experience taught me that my job was to not to give people a 'leg up', but to assess their failings, come up with a plan, then bully or cajole them into 'complying' with our directives using a carrot and stick approach. These directives were usually designed with the sole purpose of protecting children from their carers and their acts of commission or omission. As a social worker I had become an officer of the local authority, instead of walking barefoot I was wearing boots, with little understanding of how and why people change, ignorant of their strength and beauty and feeling nothing of the tender ground I walked upon.

Radical social workers argue that the profession is becoming just another way to oppress the vulnerable, policing the powerless and removing choices. I hear or read every day that social work is in crisis, it has lost its heart and soul. To a great degree I feel it has, but I am hopeful that things can change.

Organisations and their hierarchies sometimes seem more important than individuals. The individuals, the clients; the poor, weak, despised, sick, disabled, ill-educated, unemployed people who have made some unwise or even downright careless choices or who lack social, spiritual, practical or intellectual resources. These people, who are easy to oppress and discriminate against, sit right at the bottom of those hierarchies and bear their full weight. The pressure goes up through the workers and their managers, through the councillors and the government to 'public opinion' at the top, which drives the whole machine. It feels like a scared and wobbly stack which tries to create stability by controlling, and so disempowering, the layers below in a systematic way. Everybody has a tyrant on his back, and from the point of view of those at the bottom of this mountain, the tyrants seem to get more petty, more egocentric, more paranoid and damaging the further you clamber up.

I saw that system poison the workers around me. Some of them fell by the wayside, burned out after two years of child protection work, others accommodated to it, and struggled to compromise.

This system is fuelled by fear; the fear of failure, of mistakes, of the unthinkable happening, and of sensationalist media witch-hunts driven by the ignorance and self-obsession of 'public opinion'. There was a prevalent belief in childcare social work, the belief went something like this:

Childcare social work is very hard work that is emotionally demanding. Working with abused children is damaging to the worker. Working with abusers is damaging to the worker. The emotional pressures and stresses of working with abusers and abused children causes social workers to burn out.

We all accepted this and even repeated it from time to time, but really we all knew that it wasn't exactly a 100% true representation. This story is part of a 'macho' culture in childcare, which the system has an interest in maintaining. To challenge this culture would be to challenge the very basis of how systems work with individuals. Childcare social work *is* hard and demanding and it *does* burn people out, but it does so because we live with constant fear and pressure, fear of the unknown and pressure to make it safe. Furthermore we often do it with unmanageable caseloads, giving us little time to even visit clients, let alone to get to know and understand them.

You cannot be successful in any field if you work from a basis of fear. It is vital to feel competent. If you don't feel competent, you will experience emotional and psychic burnout, your fear and anxiety will consume you.

The human response to fear is to stand and fight or to run. Some workers run and take jobs elsewhere, others stay physically but run emotionally, detaching themselves from their feelings, from creativity and responsibility. Others choose to stand and fight. When they do stand and fight, their fear and their fight or flight response can result in a tendency to apply pressure to clients in the hope that they will change. If they appear to change as a result of that pressure, the workers fear can be diminished and they feel safe again. Workers do not want it to be like this, they are often just trying to cope with their fear.

If there is one thing we know about motivating people to change it is that applying pressure to an individual makes that individual resist. People want to retain their individuality, their specialness, and not be manipulated or controlled by others. When you apply pressure people may appear to change, they may play the game, but somewhere inside they retain their wonderful human spirit of independence and rebellion. They will become resistant, and resistant clients create yet more fear for workers. Clients show resistance by avoidance, by challenging the worker, by blaming other people or circumstances, by ignoring or sidetracking, by not keeping appointments, by not communicating, denying the existence of problems, going into hiding, pretending everything is alright, getting angry, misleading and being dishonest.

If a country is governed with repression, the people become depressed and crafty.

Tao Te Ching

Pressure just creates more problems for workers and for clients. You see this cycle going on all the time. When workers are afraid they try to take control and so apply pressure. When clients are under pressure, they resist. When clients resist, workers become more afraid and apply yet more pressure. Small cases result in child protection case conferences because families deny the existence of a problem. Families get taken to court for care proceedings because social workers can't get the information they need to make them feel comfortable. Workers end up feeling like petty bureaucrats, because, although they really care, they lack the resources and support they need to unlock people.

So I stopped doing social work like that and went hunting for another way of doing it. I believed that when you are able to really communicate with clients, the unknown can become the known. Fear can be diminished and even overcome. With appropriate time, resources and support from the system, we can develop relationships, and respond from an understanding of the reality of the situation rather than from a basis of fear.

A holistic approach to social work

There is a solution, a way of working that fits in with the needs of the organisations and systems which employ us and at the same time liberates workers and service users from oppression. Social work still does have a heart and soul, and we can enjoy a way of being with clients that empowers them to live the sort of lives they wish to have, rather than the ones they end up with. There is a way that social work can work far better than it does now for workers, systems and clients. I believe that we as workers can empower *ourselves* so that we can live lives where our many different roles and selves are consistent, authentic, holistic and integrated.

The importance of work itself

Work is what we do with most of our waking lives. Work is central to our happiness and our feelings of self-worth. We see ourselves reflected in our work, in the outcome and importance of what we do. When we think about our lives we often define ourselves in terms of how we make a living. We spend an enormous part of our life working, trying to make a living and trying to express our individuality. The function of work is to pay for our lives and homes and support our families, and yet employment also gives us the opportunity to express our true creative self, our individuality.

If you want to feel your life has any value, you need to consider what you do with it and how you do it. If you want to fully participate in your passing life, then you need to explore your role, your tools and resources, your place in the scheme of things. You have one precious life; what is it for and what are you going to do with it?

Is the purpose of your life to immerse yourself in problems and misery or are you doing it to creatively express yourself? Creativity is part of our human nature, yours, mine, clients, colleagues. It is at the core of how our species behaves. Our work, whatever it is that we do, is a living, growing, evolving creative activity. Even if you pluck chickens on a conveyor belt for a living, you will be driven to express your individual creativity. If employers and circumstances restrict you from doing that, the pressure of your individuality will still leak out. Human beings are animals, they naturally work; they work naturally as part of nature. They are not machines controlled by an operator. We are naturally creative, questioning creatures.

As social workers we care or we wouldn't do this kind of work, and so our caring work is a vehicle of self-expression. Our caring is personal, our creativity is our own. If you are creative, and express that creativity through caring, then you have to ask yourself how you can make things better.

The spirit in the mundane

To really understand the wholeness and meaning in people's lives we need to find the spirit in the mundane, the sacred in the ordinary, the specialness in the individual. You do this by listening with a soft ear, becoming an empty vessel and allowing people to express who they really are, in their own time, even if they sometimes don't know who they really are.

If you can find an individual's personal truth, you have the key that will unlock their creativity and allow them to flower in your hand. The essence of life is change, and so it is vital that our way of being with clients does not crush, oppress, block or restrain individual creativity and change. So professional practice becomes about waiting, listening, learning about individual human realities that are different to ours and personal to the people we are with, and then promoting their natural growth in positive directions.

Look out of your window for a tree, any tree. You can choose to see it as just a tree without paying it much attention or adding any value or description to it. A blob on the landscape. What you see depends on how you look at it, where your head is at. You could, for instance, see a tree as an individual and unique emanation of a beautiful, poetic and deeply mysterious world, a life-form that lives longer than a person, something that gives us the oxygen that we breathe, a thing that provides a home for hundreds of different species all with their own life force, a canopy or a shelter, a marker of a special place, a landmark, a beautiful object . . .

. . . Or you can see it as just another tree. Ordinary, just like all the others. And yet it is magnificent in its ordinariness.

Trees often live in forests, and one of the things that makes a forest beautiful is its variety. People live in societies, and one of the things that makes humanity beautiful also is its variety. We are all ordinary, and what makes us ordinary is the fact that each one of us is different from every single one of 6 billion others on this amazing planet. We are all extraordinary. Human beings express a phenomenal range of behaviours. We have a fantastic variety and combination of personalities, interests, values and beliefs and yet we are all normal everyday people just getting on with it. For me there is a majesty, a magnificence, a poetry in people being both ordinary and extraordinary individuals, just getting on with being themselves and living their life.

We all have strengths and weaknesses. We have a rainbow of different ideas, cultures, beliefs and idiosyncrasies. We all have personal experiences of happiness, misery, pain and success. We are all living sentient beings with personal hopes and dreams. The people we work with are the same as the people we live with, stand next to at the takeaway, share an office with, and live next door to. They are as different and as odd as we are. Left wing, right wing, Christian, Moslem, Wiccan, Buddhist, Sikh, vegetarian, bikers, rugby players, travellers, drinkers, drug users, parents and single people. All having a relationship, complex or simple, with their personal dreams and goals. All trying to deal with, accept, or overcome the obstacles (human or otherwise) that stand in their way.

We share our lives and our world, we share ideas and cultural glue. We even share the stuff our bodies are made of. The air we breathe and walk through is a soup made from the molecules from other people's bodies. When we smell the existence of another person we are breathing in the breath they have exhaled or the chemicals leaving their cells. We are closer to each other than we often like to think.

Promoting change

Social work is so often about change; promoting it, supporting it, planning it. Barefoot social work is about finding the most comfortable route to that change. A process that allows a person to be the best they can be, on their own terms and in their own context and environment. This needs to be true for workers and service users alike, and I try to draw no distinction between workers and service users. This may need a little mental gymnastics for some, we may be used to treating service users as something different from ourselves because the hierarchical systems we work and live in usually encourage that distinction.

The route to change needs to avoid harm and destruction on the way. Change should happen in a way that is sensitive to the needs of the internal personal environment of history, values and beliefs, as well as the external environment we share. Progress should concern itself with the individual human and personal circumstances that people bring with them, and it should preserve their identity, creativity and strengths as much as possible. In this way you promote growth and development instead of a total destruction, which requires a rebuilding from the ground up.

Social work is based on a simple principle – that the people who need social work intervention require it because they lack power. A social worker's role is to empower their clients. We are taught on social work courses that it is a philosophical impossibility to give power. People who are empowered take power. You cannot make people take power. You cannot make people be happy. This is a key concept in social work and yet it is so often overlooked. You cannot force power on people, you have to enable them to take power, and you cannot empower people by putting pressure on them, it has to come from inside. The social work role, therefore, is to help the individual access the strength that is inside. You do not make a plant grow by shouting at it.

I define power simply as the ability to make choices. This means the opportunity to learn, the freedom to express yourself, the strength to be happy, the resources to protect, the opportunity to earn, a sense of having some control over your own destiny, the ability to protect yourself and those more vulnerable, the opportunity to choose, the skills to fulfil your own responsibilities, the understanding to accept that there is both light and dark, the ability to change. Social work is about helping people to take down the barriers that prevent them from making these choices.

As a barefoot practitioner my ultimate goal is to leave no trace of my passing. Of course this is not always possible. I seek to help people change, but instead of imposing or demanding change, I try to catalyse it so that when I am gone, there is no trace of me, all that is left is people leading the better life they have chosen, for themselves, their children and the generations to come. Hopefully, in the years to come and by the generations that follow, all that will be remembered is family and friends who cared and did their best.

To acknowledge you need help is depressing in itself, it makes you feel powerless. It is frightening to think of people coming in to your life. The threats those people represent can be terrifying. The social work 'process' of helping is often experienced by clients as exactly the opposite.

Working in systems

As a social worker your practice is guided, instructed and framed by guidance, supervision and policy. These are things that you can, if you are so minded, put on like a pair of shoes or a uniform and use to protect and obscure the real you when working with clients. It is easy to misuse guidance and allow it take over your humanity, we see it in the actions of 'jobsworths' and unimaginative employees of powerful hierarchies every day. Work done without creativity is simply brutality.

Let me make it very clear, I am not for one moment arguing against the idea of supervision or published guidance, these frameworks are absolutely vital for your support and development, and for the safety and protection of you and your clients. But guidance is just that. You are rarely given hard uncompromising rules which you must follow, but rather a framework within which you have professional freedoms. Guidance needs to be proved or disproved, challenged and tested in the fires of practice, not followed blindly or prejudicially. It is a starting point on the road to doing your job of protecting the vulnerable and promoting their rights as individuals, a framework within which you dance your own dance. You may be a caged dancer, but the dance is completely your own. Social workers do not yet wear uniforms, we still have a chance to express our uniqueness, to use it to help others, to value diversity and challenge authority.

Any professional takes responsibility for his own practice. You are allowed to make decisions as long as you can justify them, it is what makes you a professional. So work within the rules and the frameworks, understand the guidance, but find out who **you** are. Develop you and your personal style of social work and be yourself, a magnificent individual in a forest of other magnificent individuals.

Take off your shoes, stand in the sand and look at your footprints. They are beautiful and deeply complex, individual and unlike any others. So unique you cannot stand in anybody else's footprint without damaging it. When you put your shoes back on your footprints change to one made by a factory. A footprint stamped a billion times on the earth like a rubber stamp. Commonplace, mass-produced and impersonal.

Your footprint on the world can be sensitive and is drawn from your own humanity, changing from day to day, hour to hour. Reacting to conditions, understanding and responding to the underlying texture of the environment. But it can be hard and inflexible, insensitive, unyielding, rigid, oppressive, crushing and consuming.

There is something of the artist in a good social worker. There are people who are very talented at it, others who have to work harder to achieve the same results. But any art, no matter how talented the artist, begins with awareness. Awareness is about being soft and receptive, it is a gentle process; looking with a soft eye, listening with a soft ear without judging, planning, thinking, organising or doing, just being and absorbing and eventually understanding.

Creative and engaged workers have something very clear and distinct about them, they express a love of people and a love of the millions of different ways people express their uniqueness. Some of them are quiet and thoughtful, others are more brash and noisy. Some are pushy and others more retiring. But however they do it, they know social work is about the love of humanity in all its scary guises. This love gives them a noticeable confidence.

There are plenty of social workers stomping carelessly over people's lives. I have met some, and am sure you have too. They are not like this because they are badly trained. They are, in fact (just like the people they work with and for), usually doing the best they can with the resources they have. They are not to be blamed for their lack of care, in fact they often care deeply. The simple fact is that life is a process, we are all individuals on the road, all at different places and all of us, clients and workers alike, can make use of resources that will make our lives and the lives of those around us better.

You as an individual can make things better than they are. You alone can make a difference.

Whose needs?

It often seems to me that when working with or thinking about clients, social workers ask themselves 'what needs to happen?' This question skips any attempt at real understanding and assessment. It merely asks for the worker's feelings, personal beliefs and prejudices to come into play, it presents the worker as the expert. Workers need to ask deeper questions, the answers to which demand a real understanding of the strengths within families and individuals, questions like 'What would do the least harm to this particular child?', 'What would do the most good?', 'What resources do they have?' and 'What are their strengths?'

Assessment processes are very often tick-box exercises, question and answer sessions. The agenda is an organisational one that presumes the worker is the expert. Sure, some very important questions are asked, but vital understanding of family functioning is left out. Such assessment tools promote formal question and answer sessions, leaving no room for individual creativity or skilled exploration of the family circumstances, values and strengths. Assessment processes are no substitute for good communication skills, and I believe that assessments need to be supplemented by appropriate skills which can bring forward more appropriate information than a formal structured interview ever could. For instance, I have developed a set of cards, 'Kids Need', which are used with parents and carers to look at their understanding of what children really need and explore the difference between needs and wants. Such tools automatically create a dialogue which is not threatening, but which encourages people to understand the impact of their behaviour and to challenge their own behaviour.

Assessment frameworks very often pay some kind of attention to looking for strengths, but often the strengths area of such assessment forms is left blank, or contains no detail or understanding in comparison to explorations of problems. Analysis sections too are often left blank, and so no real understanding of the wholeness and reality of the situation is gained.

Don't work too hard

While I look for a way of being in the world that creates as little damage as possible, try to experience reality, work with that reality, accept it and allow it to grow and become, thinking about how I can promote change while leaving individual functioning harmoniously and holistically rather than stained, crushed, corrupted or damaged, I am also thinking about making only as much effort as is necessary. Of doing just what needs to be done and no more.

When her work is done the master forgets it.
Do your work then step back, the only path to serenity.

Tao Te Ching

Imagine a line of footprints along a pristine beach. How beautiful, poetic, calm and relaxing the simplicity of that image is. It goes from here to there in an unbroken line, you can see clearly where it has come from and know where it is going. It is pure and obvious and human. If you stomp all over it, run around in circles, take detours here, there and everywhere, you mess it up and the feeling is gone, the image is incoherent, clumsy, complicated and meaningless; the simplicity and clarity is destroyed, as is the poetry. Simple is best. On every visit you need to have a clear sense of purpose and direction.

Many people complain that they have broken down through overwork. In the majority of such cases the breakdown is more frequently the result of foolishly wasted energy. If you would secure health you must learn to work without friction.

James Allen

Friction comes from fear borne of unnecessary pressure and lack of clarity. When you can work without applying pressure, when you can remain calm and clear about your tasks, then the whole job becomes much easier for you and for them.

Chapter 2

Relationships

Being real

Social work is about real people getting on with being people and helping others do that too. It is about life as it is lived. Real honest life with all of its grunge and shades of grey and difficulties. It is about the poetry of existence. It is about being on the edge sometimes, living and working using personal resources, creativity and love, using our values and beliefs to make the world a better place for the people we work with.

Unlike a mechanic or a builder we have few tools to rely on. You and your knowledge and wisdom are your tools, the things you use to help people. We have no clear plans that tell us part 'A' connects to part 'B' with nut 'C', we are like artists who create organically, trying something out to see if it works, changing it if it doesn't. Social work process is a creative flow. We have a 'menu' of tools and resources at our disposal, but how we use them and fit them together is entirely up to us. We can use our resources to make a tree house, a lean-to shelter or a complicated and dysfunctional mess.

Respect

It has been shown time and time again that the most therapeutic part of any therapeutic relationship is the relationship itself. Not the stuff that is done, not the therapies, but the interaction between two human beings.

The gift you offer another person is just your being.

Ram Dass

You can make people feel respected, worthwhile and hopeful, you can build trust from the very moment you meet with them. For example, being late for appointments is disrespectful and closely connected with how people perceive your power. Lou Reed in 'Waiting for my man' sings:

He's never early,
he's always late,
the first thing you learn is that you always gotta wait.

He is singing about how drug dealers express their power in this way over users. I constantly see social workers missing or arriving late for appointments with clients. To express power over people who have so little power is abusive. People who are usually late for their meetings are showing who has the power. Because they are late for you, you become late for your clients. Sadly, I also regularly see clients under the spotlight in child protection case conferences having to explain their lateness or missing appointments. There appears to be one rule for clients and another for professionals. This is a reflection of a hierarchical system where clients are at the bottom. Now, that does not make sense to me. My sole reason for being employed is to empower the most vulnerable and prioritise their needs. I should be respectful to my clients and be there when I say I will be there, others should just have to wait their damn turn. The hierarchy needs to be inverted.

Visiting people's homes

You are a visitor in people's homes. When you visit a client's home you need to be clear about your reason for being there. If you have no clear purpose in that client's home then you are just more mud on their carpet.

For many people the home is a private and sacred place, a sanctuary, a place of high emotional connection. People usually choose who they invite into their homes. If you are not to oppress or dominate it is important to treat people's homes with respect. Use your imagination to invert the process, how do you feel when an uninvited person comes to your home, how do you like to be treated?

People's homes contain personal effects, things that have meaning for the people who live there, things that they find important enough to display and live with from day to day, objects that contain history, that people use to express who they are and what they like; pictures, trophies, ornaments, wallpaper, colours, personal choices. These give real clues to the individuality of the person. Taking the time to notice these things, shows you are interested in the whole person and not just the problem, it also helps you to get a rounded picture of people's values. Ignoring personal space, going in and getting 'straight down to work' devalues their wholeness, is problem focused and so is abusive and threatening.

Trust

Sometimes I hear social workers say they can't trust clients, that drug users are all liars and so on. Even more often I hear clients say they don't trust their social workers. Both sides are completely missing the point. The role of a social worker is not to *trust*, it is to *understand*. When you understand you naturally trust people to behave in the way in which they behave. They behave in that way because that is what they know, that is how they cope. You can help them to know more and to cope better, to have more choices. That is empowerment.

When people feel that they have to mislead you, they have a reason. They may feel you do not understand the wholeness of their lives, that you only focus on the part that is worrying you, that you are not interested in, and don't appreciate, the value of the things they are doing that are strong and good and whole. They may be afraid of the consequences of being honest, or fear the worker will jump to conclusions. When people want to mislead you it is because they see you as a problem, rather than a solution. Having a client try to mislead is a clear indicator to do something differently, something that will allow them to feel they can be honest.

Of course, people sometimes have very big and serious secrets that they really want to hide because they know their behaviour is dangerous, harmful or somehow wrong, or because releasing the secret into the unknown will be too painful for them. Pressing them to tell you will not release them, only make them more afraid.

The problem of communication

Communication is fraught with difficulties. Converting our ideas into words is a complex task. Any particular idea can be expressed in a million different ways. We can never be 100% sure that what actually comes out of our mouths is what is understood by the listener, they could be placing the emphasis elsewhere and coming up with quite different meanings from those we thought we had transmitted. In normal day-to-day conversation we try to communicate with others by looking for the common ground, shared interests. It is one of the reasons we talk about the weather, we have so much of it, it is unpredictable and because of this it is a common interest that appears unchallenging. Yet different perceptions of even such a banal thing can cause us to react in unexpected ways.

I like cool dark and damp places; forests, mountainsides, beaches in the winter. I walk on the shady side of the street. I like woolly jumpers, log fires, storms, thunder and lightening, frost and cold. Heat sends me to sleep. You may like the heat; beaches, sunshine, swimming. What causes difficulty in communication is the personal value we place on information. I say it is really too hot today, you may feel it is just warm or even a little cool. Our values are as different as we are different. But we are social creatures, so when a group of us agree it is a beautiful day, some of the group just agree because that is the socially acceptable way of communicating. Clients will do this too. They will agree with you just because that is what they feel is expected of them, it is normal human behaviour.

Human verbal communication is at best a guess at what the other person means, more often it conveys no useful information at all. The most important function of normal human communication is to create 'social glue'. It is an almost automatic process to agree with other people so that we are not isolated and excluded from the tribe. I remember sitting with my grandmother and her sister when I was a child. They were two very accomplished social gluers and would both talk at the same time, neither paying attention to the other, yet both considering the other a true friend. Old ladies can be some of the most proficient and expert of social gluers.

Your professional communication, of course, needs to be of a different order than this. You are not looking solely at creating a relationship, the relationship is very important if it is to be at all helpful, but you also need other vital skills to allow the relationship to be a functional one.

Listening

Listening is a real art. In listening, the barefoot worker looks for strengths, those little seeds that can be nurtured, fed and cosseted so that they grow and become the foundation of change.

I don't know how people should live their lives, neither do you. Fortunately there is somebody who does know, the client themselves.

When you first get involved they may not think they have strengths, but they are there, and it is a social work role to help them to become aware of those strengths. Each person is an organic entity with a personality and intelligence of their own and when people become aware of their strengths, when they express them, talk about them, become clear about them and celebrate them, they begin to act upon them and make them grow. What you focus on gets bigger. The barefoot practitioner's role is to liberate the secret from the person. You are the active ingredient. Your sincerity, your intensity, your creativity, your care and your desire are the things that will make things happen.

Listening without judging

As well as looking for strengths and discussing them, barefoot workers let go of themselves. They listen, prompt and promote growth without pressure, without self, their focus remains 100% on the client and their wants, needs, strengths and opportunities for advancement.

When you make a value judgement about anything, when you add your own thoughts, you add judgement and ego which can easily block progress unless very skilfully done. Judgement is based on what information you choose to focus on and what you choose to ignore. If you want to fully experience the full majesty and complexity of any person, place, thing, meal or event you can only do it by refusing to judge or comment. Just use your eyes, your ears, your nose, your senses of taste and touch. Become open and aware, switch on your senses and switch off your constant internal dialogue. When you do this with people they can begin to risk themselves a little and become free of the fear of being judged, and when people feel free to risk themselves, they rehearse their goals and skills and they begin to change.

Change and growth take place when a person has risked himself and dares to become involved with experimenting with his own life.

Herbert Otto

Paraphrasing

Good communication skills are very powerful, they help people to feel in charge of their lives, they let the person know you are listening and trying to understand, they help the individual to feel their position is valued. People begin to understand that they are the expert on the detail of their lives and begin to come up with their own solutions, their confidence increases and their strength to risk change grows.

One of the greatest communication skills is the ability to paraphrase what an individual is saying. When somebody says something, repeat it back to them just as they sent it to you, so they understand that you have heard and understood what they are trying to tell you and will elaborate. In this way you and they slowly build up a picture of what they are trying to express, and they will understand that you are interested and that you are listening. If they disagree with your reflection, they will put you straight, if they agree, they will elaborate. This is a soft and gentle process.

If we start to pull this together, including your search for strengths and the seeds of growth, you can easily imagine a scenario which goes something like this much condensed example:

I am very angry with him
You are angry with him
Yes, because he won't do what I tell him
When you tell him to do things he won't do them
Yes
What kind of things won't he do?
He won't go to school
You want him to go to school
Yes, but he won't listen to me
He doesn't listen to you
Well sometimes he does, but not always
What things does he listen to you about?
Well, he comes in when I ask him to and he helps with housework –
but that is because he likes cooking
He likes cooking
Yes, he is very creative
And he comes in when you want him to?
Yes, but he won't go to school
What would help him to go to school
If people would leave him alone, teachers and other kids

In real life progress would not be so quick, but I think it gives a taste of how some simple paraphrasing, with the odd solution focused question thrown in, moves the client from saying they are angry because the child will not do as they are asked to acknowledging that sometimes the child will do as they are asked even if they don't want to. It becomes clear that the problem is not that the child will never do as they are asked, but that the carer has focused on this one issue and generalised it.

Beginning with valuing and validating the client's concerns and worries and allowing them to express those feelings, quickly and easily moves on to exploring strengths and then solutions.

Inevitably, during this process, your mind will start to try to formulate solutions; anti-bullying tactics, changing schools, talking to the teachers or working with the child to address his confidence. Don't go diving in too soon with solutions. If you dive in too soon the client will feel you are not valuing their concerns. Clients' concerns and fears need to be acknowledged, respected and accepted as part of the wholeness of the individual, but yet not increased by the worker's focus upon them. This is a delicate balancing act.

If you use listening and paraphrasing skills you will very quickly discover what the problems are and what resources the individual has to begin to deal with them. This is not a process of interviewing, but of interacting. It is a two way process, where sometimes the client leads and sometimes the worker, but always looking for strengths. Out of those strengths will come solutions. You need to continue this process until the client comes up with their own solutions.

If you do this well the client will come to know several things very quickly; you are not just hearing them but are actively listening and giving them your full awareness and attention, and analysing, interpreting, and understanding what they are saying to you. They then become convinced that you are interested in them, and care about them and that you are a very understanding person. They also quickly become aware that they do have skills and resources, their confidence grows and creative change is then fuelled.

Finding the truth

The next few paragraphs are drawn extensively from my previous book, *Preventing Breakdown* and so I must apologise for repeating it here if you have read that book. I felt that it was important to explore this again in the context of this work.

The truth consists of the whole truth, not just selected parts of it. In other words not just the bad, weak, shameful stuff but the strong, positive and hopeful stuff as well. If you take sections of the truth out of context (positive or negative) they cease to be a real representation and become a biased personal interpretation. If you focus on the problems more than the strengths then you do not see the whole truth, and when families become aware of the problem-focused nature of the worker they begin to lose trust, their desire to communicate fades and they become resistant.

The only people who know the whole truth are the family members and so your job is to listen to the wholeness of the truth from your clients, and not just to learn, but to understand what their story means to each of them, not what it means to you, but what it means to them. What the problems mean in the context of their strengths, personality, spirituality and beliefs. What their strengths mean in the context of their problems. You and your clients working together can make and share accurate assessments and develop intervention strategies which are useful to them as people.

Workers routinely come across family members who have a whole variety of problems and difficulties; emotional problems, parenting skills, anger management, heroin addiction, alcohol misuse, domestic violence, depression, agoraphobia, physical disability and any number of aspects of human behaviour and lifestyle that have an impact on the person's ability to be whole. Workers cannot be experts on every kind of problem they are likely to come across. To attempt to assess on your own how each problem impacts on the individual and the family is fraught with difficulties. Any such problem will affect each individual differently. People go through different stages and cycles dependant upon a whole variety of factors; age, emotional state, time of the year, the weather, and what happened this morning. Each difficulty is unique to the individual who has it, and its effect on family members is different for each member at different times.

It is therefore not the problem that is specialised, it is the individual. It is a fundamental practitioner skill to engage and understand a client, to work in partnership with the client and to accept them as an expert on their situation. I cannot stress enough that the worker's role is to learn from the client. People living with the problem have more knowledge of the problem than any expert. Their in-depth knowledge is born from living with it day after day, it underlies every other thing that they do in their lives. It is there when they go to bed and when they get up in the morning. They know what has worked in the past and what hasn't worked. They know what other people feel they 'should' try, they know what they have tried and what they don't feel capable of trying. They know it all backwards, forwards and inside out. They know what physical, emotional and spiritual resources they have and, with your support, they will come up with creative ideas about what might help in the future. If you let people come up with their own solutions, they come up with solutions that fit their needs.

Who is the client?

Throughout this book I talk about clients, how you communicate with them, how you can empower them to make changes in their lives. When I speak of clients I am talking about the individual or group that you are currently attempting to communicate with in the context of your enabling work. In childcare we are supposed to be 'child-centred', the child is considered to be the client and although much of our time will be spent communicating with their parents and carers and motivating or enabling them to make positive changes, we do not usually consider them to be our clients. This is clearly wrong. The client is the person or group in whom you are attempting to influence change. In child care work, the case file may be in the child's name, the client is clearly the family as a group and each member of that family as individuals.

Working with risk

To assess risk, to plan interventions, to develop rapport and to work in partnership with individuals, workers must watch and listen without coming to early judgements or conclusions. With an open state of mind, a worker can ask questions that inspire hope that things can improve and encourage people to come up with their own solutions.

The nature of social work is risk, we work with it every day, we have to be comfortable with it, negotiate and embrace it and at the same time to focus on success. Risk exists and will not go away. Trying to make risk go away hurts people and results in intrusive and unnecessary state intervention in family life. Confidence in dealing with risk comes with clarity and understanding of the reality of the situation. Which risks are real and which are more imagined? In order to make such assessments workers and clients need to communicate and workers need to be aware.

People are usually doing the best they can from their level of awareness. Except in the rarest of cases, parents don't usually want to abuse their children. When people get it wrong it is usually out of a lack of personal, spiritual, or emotional resources, an inability to control anger, frustration, an inability to cope. Some of the things people do may be unpleasant to your eyes, sometimes their behaviour will be oppressive, abusive and dangerous to others and you may need to remind yourself that who they are and how they behave are two completely different things. Your role is to provide them with better tools and skills, but if this is not possible or appropriate perhaps to take legal action.

Working with risk is particularly difficult. If, for instance, you are working with a family where many indicators and behaviours point to children being abused, yet no physical evidence has been obtained, when you have to make that horrendous decision based on the balance of probabilities which is allowed for in the Children Act, you can, using this barefoot philosophy, at least gain a more holistic view of family functioning and give people a real opportunity to engage with you and gain more appropriate skills. Should they fail to do so, you will have the confidence that comes with the knowledge that you have done all that you can.

Things going wrong

Our culture focuses on things going wrong. Even when things are looking good with a client or family it can be tempting to remind everybody of the risks and past problems. Your ability to create a balance and keep these issues on the table in a solution-focused way depends on your confidence, skill, the support you have and your current emotional state.

Such a task might seem to be mind-blowingly complicated, but we are provided with a raft of tools to help us to make assessments and provide interventions. I provide some tools in my last book (mentioned earlier) but it is not merely the tools that do the job. A chisel is no use in the hands of somebody who does not know how to use it, it just becomes a weapon, and so a theory, some philosophy to work by, is important.

Any craftsman or artist approaches his work as an empty vessel. You cannot force a block of stone to take on a shape that its internal nature will not allow it to take, all you will do is destroy the stone due to its hidden flaws. You do not know what its internal nature is until you find it, so you approach the work empty, perhaps with a few vague ideas, and allow the form to reveal itself. Sculptors talk of not forcing a carving to take a shape, but of gently releasing the form from the stone. This mindset is a very valuable asset in a social worker.

Later on in this book we will look at how you can experience being an empty vessel, without internal dialogue and how to be rid of preconceptions and prejudices. But before that we will look at how you can avoid breaking the stone, allowing the perfect form to reveal itself and become self-determining. Creating change in people without crushing or damaging their human spirit or energy.

Chapter 3

Creating Change

Valuing individual creativity

When people find their own path they follow it. Of course, valuing people's uniqueness does not mean that it is okay for those unique people to oppress, abuse, hurt, exploit or damage the lives of others. And sometimes you have to give information so that people can make choices. But when you do, you need to be aware that when there is such a massive power imbalance, any information may be seen by the recipient as a directive. As already discused, directives create resistance. So use them at your peril.

Social work is often about dealing or working with conflict. Social work values are about helping clients to achieve freedom from oppression, whether it is external or internal. Clients want the same things as you. Parents don't usually want to abuse their children and children don't want to be neglected. Social workers and families often want the same things, yet it often feels like we are in conflict with parents. How does this come about?

Conflict comes from having personal opinions or ideas about how things 'should' be. Human beings can become frustrated when their ideas are not the same as those of others and they may try to press their ideas upon each other.

When we try to press our beliefs on another person, it is really a reflection of ourselves, clearly indicating that we have not allowed the other person to truly open up to us and tell us who they really are. We have not experienced their 'specialness'. When you apply pressure to people they hide their true selves from you and you don't get a balanced picture. When you try to press your ideas on another, even at the low level of giving friendly advice, you deny the individual the use of their personal creativity. Giving advice is more often disabling than it is enabling. If you do people's thinking for them you deny them the opportunity to be creative, develop and think for themselves. You become an 'expert' who has all the answers and so undermine people in subtle ways, ultimately making them dependant.

Sometimes people will ask for advice, but their request is not an offer to follow your advice, they are looking for alternatives from which they will make their own choice based on the facts at their disposal.

You have a case file, and may be well aware of concerns from the past, be it recent or distant, and you may be bursting to instruct people not to behave in that way again. As we shall see, there are ways of addressing those issues which allow people to move forward and other ways of communicating which will freeze their progress, throw them into guilt or fear and make them view you as a problem rather than a solution.

Human beings crave independence, to be in control of their lives as much as they are capable. Clients, just like the rest of us, want happiness and success, but most of all they want to feel good about themselves, so that for me is the starting point. Social workers often talk about people being the experts on their situation, we need to put this idea into practice, to work with the individual on their terms, in their context, with their hopes, dreams and beliefs, so that in the end they can say 'I did it using my own strengths and resources' instead of feeling that something was done to them. In this way they own the life they have created, they are responsible for it and have the ability to change it. They have learned they have the power, the ability and the confidence to make their world different so that when in the future they are challenged by circumstances, they do not blindly cry for help but take action and make changes.

Sometimes people seem to want you to be the expert, seem to be asking for a miracle worker to come in to the family and cure everybody. When this happens it is easy to get involved in a very interesting cycle. There is a great desire in all of us to come up with helpful suggestions, it inflates the ego and makes us feel good. So when people try to get you to rescue them, your ego will get all puffed up and think 'aha, here's my chance to feel good about myself'. You get hooked in and start to look for solutions. You may come up with an idea, they tell you that sounds like a really good idea and they will try it. Strangely, when you go back and ask the client how it went, they tell you that for some reason it didn't work because: 'Martin didn't listen, Jenny just laughed at me, I couldn't remember what I was supposed to do, I lost my purse, the bus didn't come' or any number of more or less creative reasons why your solution didn't work.

The response to your suggestions could also be more blatant: 'I tried that before' or 'that would never work', or 'they would never listen', or any number of reasons for your suggestions not being appropriate, useful or practical. Their manner is 'OK Mr clever clogs, Expert, see what wonderful ideas you can come up with now to sort this out!' You end up feeling they do not really want your help. In fact it appears that they are using you to support their inability to make changes. As if to get you to say 'Poor you, there is no cure, it must be awful for you'.

People crave independence, but they are capable of tricking themselves into thinking that they already have independence, and, even with their independence, there is no cure for their ills, clever wonderful creative creatures that they are. They do not want your cures, that would make them dependant. They want your cures to fail so that they are justified in their failing. When somebody wants you to be an expert it is just bait on a hook and, at the end, your hungry ego will make you look arrogant and silly.

When you are more forceful, and strongly suggest people make changes that are not their own, they will resist, and so work can start to feel like the meeting of dumb pressure and stubborn resistance. If you tell people where to go and what to do, you are doomed to fail. If you push against somebody they will naturally push back. If you give instructions on how to behave without reference to their own wishes, they will be driven to express their independence and want to react by doing the opposite, even if they know it is wrong or harmful or they may not act upon the impulse, they may in fact agree to follow your advice, but will feel frustrated and crushed and want you to get out of there so they can get on with their lives. Let's be honest, when a social worker gives advice, no matter how gently that advice is phrased, the client will often see it as a threat. Advice does not use their skills or their abilities, advice simply says:

> I think you should do it this way and I have all the power, so if you don't follow my advice you could be in real trouble.

The barefoot worker enlightens, develops choices and enables people to express their own desire to go in a more positive direction. Progress flows from working with your clients, using your combined creativity and compassion rather than battering against a hard and unyielding enemy. We are not there to impose our beliefs on anybody, we are there to help our clients function to the best of **their** ability. They need to be able to sustain any change after you have gone therefore it has to be a change that they have decided to make, not your change that you have pressured them to make. Of course, there will always be conflict in this weird profession, we may have different ideas about childcare for instance, but it is clear that the social worker's role is not to oppress, but to teach and learn in a spirit of partnership. It can be as simple as deciding not to give instructions:

You need to make sure that he gets up for school in the morning

but asking questions instead:

In what way would you like to be a better parent. What would you like to be different? How could you do that? What would help you?

Effective social work treads lightly on human lives and spirits. Communication that is effective is graceful and effortless, there is no resistance and no pressure. If our words come from the intellect and the depths of our humanity, instead of from our more damaging and superficial emotions like fear, anger and ego, then work flows naturally from our compassion, from our love and from our being, it becomes an effortless and graceful flow; work but somehow not work, progress without undue effort. If you feel the universe is working against you – it is you who are working against the universe. Accept what is and work to create what could be.

Life is about change, from one moment to the next, one day to the next, one year to the next, a process of becoming that which you are not yet. It is a journey rather than a destination. But sometimes you can be stuck in a station or at roadworks, or waiting for a bus for quite a long time. Change can also be painful. Move a baby from a warm place to a cold one and it will cry. Lose a partner and you will be in pain. We all know that moving house is one of the most stressful events that humans experience.

If you are going to be of help to other people you must first be able to see the human-ness of what they are doing, who they are and what their problems are. People are usually doing the best they can with their ability, their level of awareness and their understanding. Sometimes they do not understand the breadth and depth of their actions, but you can help them to do this by helping them to talk about their wishes and dreams for their families and their future.

Change is a natural process

Life is a torrent of creative energy, it pushes the trees out of the ground and the rain from the sky. This energy creates the diversity of insects and plants and makes people have sex, paint pictures and campaign for or against the building of a shopping centre or football ground. You can stay away, fear and avoid the river of life's turbulence, you can dip your toe into the torrent or paddle in the shallows, you can throw caution to the winds and plunge in up to your neck or you can sit on the bank and enjoy watching it dance by. I guess you, like me, know people who have been comfortable living in each of these different places.

Human life is a journey, like a leaf on a river. On the tree you were just part of the tree, without any separate identity. By falling from the tree, you begin a new and separate existence, an individual floating on the river. We find ourselves surrounded by many others floating on their part of the river, some of them may be from our tree, most of them from other trees. Some arrived before us, some arrive after us. Over time as we journey, we see many things, have collisions with other leaves, see new ones arrive and old ones disappear, and as more time passes we become harder and less flexible, battered by the waves, we gradually change from soft and supple to wrinkly and stiff and eventually our journey through this life ends and our bodies decay and go back to the soil where they came from. The river of life and its many other travellers journey on without us.

Individual life flows from birth to death, you start fresh and clean at a particular place and time, then go places. During the journey life changes, becomes something else, something more earthy, then it ends. You can't get off; you can't change lives, you can't go back to the beginning. You can't explore the source of the river of life, that is mere speculation, as are ideas about where it ends up, if it ever does. Just the here and now, your time, your place, your milieu, your individuality. And that is where you must do your work and explore your life, in the here and now, with the situations that present themselves to you.

Some people's lives flow nice and easy from beginning to end. Some places in the river are wide, shallow, warm and slow, other places are freezing fast torrents with rocks and dangerous places. You have no control of when or where you were born and little over the currents that try to move you from a nice place to a difficult one, or vice versa.

Imagine a leaf floating on a pool, in a small eddy at the side of the river. A natural place where rocks have trapped the water. The leaf floats round, journeying nowhere it hasn't been before, just turning around and around in lazy circles seeing nothing new, nothing changes. The leaf just gets older, decays. Sometimes life does this to people, gets stuck and goes nowhere, we just go round and round doing the same old thing, sitting in that one place while our time on this earth passes and we get older, drier, wrinklier and closer to the end of our personal journey.

Other people seeing this may feel the need to help us to move on, to rescue us. But that in itself could be risky. If they make lots of noise and waves, carelessly splashing about, they risk sinking us altogether. Life is tough as leather and as delicate as blossom at the same time, it is driven to survive and yet can be dashed out of your body by the slightest impact or smallest of microbes. That is the beauty and the poetry of life.

If you wanted to help the leaf move on and escape the trap, you could get involved, get wet, get into some major damn-construction, or take the leaf out, wade somewhere else and gently let it go. You could stand at the bank, stay dry and throw rocks into the water near the leaf. If you were so minded you could even try using willpower, or shouting at the leaf, telling it to move back into the river. Whatever you tried, helping that leaf to move on could take a lot of effort and easily risk sinking the leaf altogether depending on how buoyant it is.

Helping is a risky business

When you intervene you take risks with other people's lives. You need to ask why you are helping at all. Are you doing it for the sake of your ego? For money? Because you empathise and you don't want others to suffer the same way you suffered? Is helping really the right thing to do? What are you risking for the client? What is to be gained? What is to be lost? And what is the most helpful thing you can do? Sometimes people do not want your help, what do you do then? Sometimes the best thing you can do is to leave people alone to sort it out for themselves.

I believe in the essential and subversive and revolutionary nature of human love. We can begin our revolution by exploiting each other less today; by avoiding manipulative devices however difficult that may be in a society which treats people as industrial units rather than as human beings.

David Brandon

Helping needs to come from a place where you and the client are the same. You cannot be separate and 'manage' people's situations. But you can join with, understand and support people to access their strengths. When we are stuck and open to help, we need somebody who will be sensitive to our delicate life, help us get back into the flow while at the same time allowing us to take our own route. The last thing we need is somebody standing on the banks shouting at us to move and throwing rocks at us.

To help people back into the mainstream you need to redirect the energy spent going round in circles. Moving people on sometimes feels like breaking a trance; talking about things other than the pain they are preoccupied with; having people tell you about their balance, what is good, as well as what is bad, what is light instead of what is dark, what is working rather than what isn't. Pay attention to the other side of the scales.

Ask them what would be bad about giving up a bad thing and what would be good about giving up a bad thing. Or what would be good about giving up a good thing and bad about giving up a good thing. Explore, expose and discuss the whole multi-dimensional reality of the situation. Allow them to discover their own balance. Allowing them to express themselves. Give people the opportunity to be aware of their own harmony or disharmony. Without advice or control, just invite contemplation by asking the questions.

Give yourself up to whatever the moment brings. Wait for the right action to present itself, the solution to appear from the client's lips then grab it with both hands. If it struggles then it was not the right action. Let go and wait for the next wave. Do not back your client into a corner and leave them without choices. Lead them to making their own choices from their own solutions. Give them the opportunity to provide solutions. If you use threats, bullying or coercion, this will be seen for what it is and will drive your client into a defensive attitude. Force or pressure are the tools of fear and peace is of the highest value.

Motivation and confidence

To create change in clients, first of all you need to become detached from it, forget what changes you would like to see for a while so that you are not tempted to impress your ideas on others. They may well come up with something far better. Your ego is an unnecessary encumbrance to you in this situation and, more importantly, to your client. You need to be calm, an empty vessel without any attachment. Whether you act or not, things will change because that is the nature of life. Whatever you choose to do may or may not have an effect in moving that change in a preferred direction. With this level of detachment you will be flexible and prepared to help people to identify areas where they are able to change in positive and creative ways.

Changing your life can be very difficult, even when it is really important that you do it. Most people choose to carry on just as they are until something forces them to change. Human change requires two properties, confidence and motivation. If people feel confident that they could change if they wanted to but they don't want to, then they will not change. Conversely, if they feel it is important to change but believe that change is not possible, they will not change. It is important for confidence and motivation to be there.

In order to change people need to have those two vital qualities. They need to want to change, to see the need, to be motivated. They also need to feel confident that they are able to do it.

The equation is simple really:

$$\text{Motivation} + \text{Confidence} = \text{Change}$$

The equation may be simple, but like all equations the underlying reality is not so simple. If either of the two factors of motivation and confidence are lacking, then change will not happen. It can take a lot of effort for people to find either of those two factors:

- Confidence comes from believing that you have the skills to do something and from previous success in doing it. Often it is the lack of confidence, hope and skills that gets people into trouble in the first place.

- Motivation comes from a vision of a better future or wanting to avoid an unpleasant one. Often there are elements of both.

In order to help another person you need a very light touch. As a worker you can build on another human being's confidence or you can crush it, you can build on their motivation and raise their excitement about a better future or you can cause people to avoid all thoughts of the future and entrench themselves in a dysfunctional present.

You cannot force people to be motivated or to be confident in their ability to change. Confrontation only makes such situations worse. If you confront and pressure people with the need to change they can crumble and feel even more hopeless, unskilled and useless. They may express this in defiance, resistance, avoidance, suicide threats, deep depression, aggression and any number of coping behaviours that mammals use when under pressure to do something they feel they can't.

Both confidence and motivation are rooted in the imagination: so you have to work with the imagination to change them.

Fortunately there are tools that can help you to do this. You will find them in Motivational Interviewing and Brief Solution Focused Therapy and in the rest of this book.

Being solution focused

Patanjali, the author of the Yoga Sutras and the father of Yoga (my favourite of the barefoot arts) believed that what you focus on in life gets bigger.

Let me say it again in really big letters because this is extremely important:

What you focus on gets bigger

Solution focused therapy has this concept as its backbone. What you pay attention to tends to grow. You will also come across this idea if you read any yoga philosophy, Taoism or Buddhism. The idea has migrated across to a lot of new age stuff around creative visualisation, and you will find it if you read anything about pagan and magical belief systems. This has been heavily researched and proven as a core concept of brief solution focused therapy and cognitive behavioural therapy (CBT), neuro linguistic programming (NLP), hypnotherapy and life coaching.

Each of these traditions has its own theories about why what you pay attention to should actually get bigger. I remember as a child my father bought a Volkswagen Beetle. Driving along, I began to notice lots of other Beetles. Thousands of them, the world was full of them and I had never even noticed them before. The same happens if you have a baby, you suddenly see millions of babies.

The mechanism here is simple to understand. When you are unfamiliar with something, when it has no meaning for you, you are less likely to notice it, but when you are aware that something is possible for you, then it is more likely to happen. When Roger Bannister broke the four-minute mile, the impossible suddenly became possible and athletes were running four-minute miles all over the damn place.

This is important for you and your clients. If you are not expecting or ready for success, you are not likely to see it. If you feel without hope, you are less likely to notice or accept the reality of successful events when they happen and more likely to dismiss success when you see it.

It helps to have a clear idea of what success looks like. Doing creative work with the client can help both of you to be clear about what the signs of success are and prepare you both for dealing with it when it first raises its tiny paw, rather than dismissing it and letting it die. We will look at this in more detail later.

In the sort of human behaviour change that we, as social workers or helpers, are interested, success will at first be just a tiny sign. People usually, but not always, change in small increments. They tentatively try things out to see if they work. Change will probably be tiny and tentative, you need to be ready to pounce on it and big it up when you see it.

When you visit a client you inevitably have an agenda, that is (hopefully) to help them on the road to living the kind of lives they hope to live. You need to listen carefully; develop a radar for positive statements, hopeful solutions, ways forward. You can support these statements by engaging when you hear them, allowing negative, hopeless statements to go by without focussing on them or reinforcing them in any way and by working with positives, asking questions about positives and quietly accepting the negatives.

When you work in this way the relationship becomes a very powerful one. You cease to be worker and client, the distinction fades away, and a true partnership emerges, two human beings working together with the same goal in mind. You become a force for good in the individual's life, a useful and positive resource. Of course this is not about being some pie-in-the-sky Pollyanna. You are not pretending that everything is just fine and dandy, but you are choosing to put some weight on the positive side of the scales, and so give some strength and capacity back to the individual. They already know all the crappy stuff. They have had it reinforced time and time again by professionals and by themselves. The barefoot worker adds balance and promotes growth and so builds confidence and motivation.

The importance of feeling positive

The greatest thing you can take away from this book is not the words, but the 'feeling'. In all helping relationships 'feeling' is a tool. We are all aware that feelings are 'catching', moods can be influenced automatically and unknowingly. Feelings leap from one person to another; evoking tenderness, inciting shame, igniting rage, exciting fear. They can be catching in one to one situations and in groups, one person can affect a group and a group can affect an individual. We are empathic creatures, advertising relies on this to induce us to feel good about the products they want us to buy, music relies on this to manipulate our emotions.

A social worker who feels a situation is hopeless is not going to add anything positive to a family's ability to improve their situation. They will pass that feeling of hopelessness on to their client and can only do more harm than good. Feeling without hope makes success far less likely and you will fail to see or enable appropriate solutions. If you feel positive, honest and hopeful then you will automatically pass this on to your clients. Without their knowing why, the people you work with will be happier, more motivated and more confident in your abilities and in their own, just because you feel positive about the potential for growth.

Work with positives

Very early on in your work with families, usually on the fist visit there will be an outpouring of problem talk. This is what they know and what their lives have consisted of up to this moment. It is very important when people focus on negatives that you allow them to express their feelings. You need to let people continue speaking and get their feelings out, accept that their fear, anger and sadness are valid. This can be relieving and cathartic for them. Often they pour it out then become calm, relieved that it has gone and somebody has listened. The workers task here is to reflect content and feelings but also look out for positives, don't reinforce problem talk but validate feelings while looking for strengths:

That must have been very hard for you, how on earth did you cope?

As you begin to explore how they coped and begin to talk about strengths, you can ask them what they like about their home, the area they live in, their family, their children, their eldest child, next child etc. What they like about themselves.

People will often feel a little confused by this, it is not what they are expecting. Very often clients themselves have become overly attached to the problem, balance has disappeared and they can no longer see goodness, solutions or anything positive about their life. Some will want to continue to tell you about problems e.g. When you ask what they like about child 'A' they might say, 'Nothing, she is a monster and I want her taken away'. You could explore a little further:

So tell me what is good about her? (looking for positives)
Nothing, she is a cow.
You are annoyed at her? (Validating feelings)
Yes, I am. I just want her out.
(pause)
Sometimes it's difficult. (Validating feelings)
Yes.
And sometimes not so difficult? (Looking for positives)
Sometimes.
So when it is difficult, how do you cope? (Looking for positives and potential solutions)
I just try to ignore her.
It helps to get some space between you and her? (Looking for potential solutions)
Yes.
There are times when things are not so difficult?
I suppose so.
What is it like then?
She used to get herself up to go to school on her own.
She sorted herself out in the morning?
Oh yes, she got up and dressed and got to school.
And you would like to it be like that again?

Yes.
What else would you like to be different?
Well, I would like her to come in on time and not be so rude.
You would like her to get herself to school, come in on time and not be so rude. It sounds like you care for her very deeply.

You need to be looking for positives all the time. Don't labour it, there is no point going in with the idea that everything is hunky-dory when it clearly isn't. They will just think that you are a nutter and that you are not listening. What you are doing is looking for balance and trying to get the person to see that there are some strengths, that it is not all bad. With an awareness of balance, they can begin to explore some potential solutions.

When you explore solutions with clients, the problems are taken for granted. Problems become part of the exploration, the balance of their wholeness, and not the sole focus of the exploration. This is wholistic social work. The individual becomes a whole person rather than a problem. You become aware of the whole situation, you understand it more. The client feels valued and important, strengths are recognised and accessible, can be used by the client to challenge their problems. Clients become motivated, encouraged and confident in their ability to do something about the problems. If you focus on problems, however, the opposite applies. The problem gets fed, grows and becomes an enormous monster in everybody's perceptions, hiding the solutions.

Being solution-focused builds hope and confidence that things can get better, creates an atmosphere of progress and forward looking and also creates motivation to change, because it focuses on how life could be so much better.

All around us, in shop windows and magazines, we see adverts for solutions; 'meal solutions', 'IT solutions', 'holiday solutions', marketing solutions', sleeping solutions', 'travel solutions'. These ready-made, off-the-shelf, one-size-fits-all solutions arise out of somebody focussing on a clear and defined problem. (The problem nearly always is; 'How can we sell more stuff to these goons?')

I don't do problems or solutions, I let my clients do that. Trying to create solutions can easily end up creating more problems. If you aspire to a life that is creative and self-expressive, then so do your clients. Life is not a problem to be solved but a natural ongoing process, doing your work is not mere problem solving, it is the art of creative living, the natural function of a creative living being. We are interested not in the solution of a single problem, but in helping the individual to express themselves creatively and constructively so that they can develop their own solutions and move on. If all you do is look for a solution to your understanding of somebody else's problem, that is all you will come away with, *your* solution, that the other person may or may not have any faith in.

Sometimes the people we work with have been crushed by problems and can see no solutions of their own. Very often they feel worn out, frightened and angry. These feelings prevent them from acknowledging their strengths. They become unable to figure out what to do next, and are unaware of their resources. To come up with solutions they need to feel hopeful, creative, positive, worthwhile and independent. If they feel without hope, they will not change. To help them to solve their problems you need to help people to get comfortable with the feeling of hope and discover how to use that hope to get creative. It is the worker's task to bring these resources to the surface, to acknowledge and celebrate them.

Work in the present

All that you have is the present, and it is important to work in the moment with whatever tools you are provided with. If you stay focused on the here and now of a situation, things can be changed from moment to moment. The present is the most powerful thing you have. This present, and the next present and all the following presents lead to one of a multitude of destinations. However, you have no control whatsoever over the outcome of your work or people's choices. What you decide to do now may well make the future change, but not in any predictable way.

> *Man can (and does) choose what causes he shall set in operation, but he cannot change the nature of effects; he can decide what thoughts he shall think and what deeds he shall do, but he has no power over the results of those thoughts and deeds . . . Man has all power to act, but his power ends with the act committed. The result of the act cannot be altered, annulled or escaped; it is irrevocable.*

> James Allen

People and other things change over time. The only thing that is permanent in this life is change. If you work with people in the context of their past failings they will be resentful and resistant to you. It is natural that they should be so. If, however, you work with them in the context of future successes they may develop dreams and fantasies that can build confidence and be motivators for change. But change can only take place in the present. Plans for the future are worth nothing unless they are put into action in the present. What concerns most service users is their personal present. Life can be so hard that all they can do is try to deal with what is happening now, at this moment. The future and past are largely irrelevant.

Sometimes clients can be fixated on things that have happened in the past and you may need to help them focus on the present. They need help to put their baggage down for a while and look around to see where they really are. People will often explain what is happening in the present in terms of what happened in the past. They talk about blame, hurt and history. The past is called the past for good reason, it has passed, and you can't go backward and do it all again. But you can change the present. It is important that people be allowed to express themselves and when they express their fixation with the past you need to allow them time and space to do this, but your role is to gently guide them back onto talk of the present and the future in a solution focused way:

It sounds like that was a very difficult time, and it seems to have affected the way you feel about things today. What ideas and thoughts help you to keep going?

Life goes by like a rollercoaster, you can either experience it or you can watch it, is your choice. But whatever you do, it goes by, you can't stop it or send it back to the beginning. Unfortunately, as far as we know, you can't get back on again at the end and do it again. You have to learn from your mistakes and use your knowledge in this life.

It doesn't matter where an individual starts from, that is just the back-story, unchanging and unchangeable history. Everybody has experienced successes and failures, been places, done things, had things done to them, hurt and been hurt, seen joy and pain. They are the stories that makes each of us into the unique individuals that we are, no better, no worse, but special in our own individuality.

We head toward the future, and that future is affected, created and developed in a complex way by the subtle things that happen now, by the things we do and feel, by the way we choose to react, by what we prefer to believe. The future and the past both grow out of the present. A present lasts from moment to moment, it is now . . . and now . . . and now . . . The outcome of all those passing moments is so complex we have no control over how they develop into our future. At this time the future is no more than a fantasy.

If you can improve on the present you can improve life.

Paulo Coelho

Exploring who people really are

Clients bring their knowledge of the problem. Their knowledge of themselves, their family, their resources, their community, their hopes and dreams, their strengths, personal and family values, their knowledge of the genesis of the problem, of its history, of successes and failures in dealing with it. These are the things that make us strong as individuals, that make us different from each other, that feed our creativity and make us special. It is vital that you use this knowledge if you are going to have any positive effect. Sometimes just exploring these things can change a situation drastically.

To use this inner strength you need to make yourself into a mirror. You need to allow the person to see and acknowledge the positive things about themselves and realise that when they do this they can grow strong, balance can be restored and they can be whole again. The important thing is to get involved in what makes each of us unique, what is important and what our dreams are for the future. It can be easy to start this process off if you are observant. Have a quick look around the space you are in, the individual's home. Although homes can be very poor there are often items which can give a clue; photographs, ornaments, pictures, unusual objects, trophies and so on. You will need to lead the session, and it must be treated more like a conversation than an interview, relaxed, friendly and open giving the client no sense of being assessed:

That's an interesting picture, lovely blues in it, do you like it?
What does it say to you?

It seems very relaxing to me, peaceful, how do you feel about it?
What else do you like about your home. What things are special to you.
Why are they special?

You are not looking for stock answers, you are exploring their deep and meaningful truths. So if they mention, in the context of the picture that you spoke about, that they like the colour red, they might be telling you that they like it because it is strong and vibrant, and you can get into a conversation about why they like strong and vibrant things and what is strong and vibrant about them, or what colour they feel now and what colour they would like to feel and what that means and how they could do it.

Look for the deepest most strongly held beliefs your client has. You need to find out what their beliefs about family life are, what they value in life. What are their aspirations? If they started off being resistant, saying nothing needed to change, they would soon realise that things can always get better. They need to be doing all the work; expressing, confirming their beliefs, turning them into positive statements, making them real.

Move on to talk about what people believe, ask about their spiritual beliefs, ask about who is important, what things are important to them. Be creative:

What do you think is important in life in terms of who makes the rules in the home?
So what are your feelings about how children should be disciplined?
What would be the right thing to do about it?
Who is the best cook in the house, what do you like to cook?
Who is the strongest?
Who is the happiest?
Who is the most talented?

This is a gentle and relaxed process, people see you are a human being with feelings too and not just an officer. You are forming a helping relationship, and while it may be true the relationship may last for no more than one or two visits, during that time you will get deeper, you will feel less stressed, they will feel less stressed and more open and honest, they will feel that you at least are interested, are bothered about who they are, they may even feel that you actually care. You are showing you believe that what they have to say is important, this makes them, as individuals, feel acceptable and shows that you are gentle, can be trusted and will not impose your own beliefs. Most importantly, it shows you are willing to treat them as another human being who knows what they are talking about. This is the foundation for a healing relationship that builds confidence, self-esteem, personal effectiveness and real change.

What you will also get is tons and tons of motivational information about how this individual wants to live their life and what they want to be different. You will become clear about their understanding of what the problems are and at the same time what they feel their resources are to deal with them.

You need to take your time over this, and to be there for as long as it takes, setting the tone for future communication. This can be very disarming for clients who may have had bad experiences with social workers, who may have problems trusting and who may be totally focused on problems and out of reach of solutions.

Communication at this level is about listening with a soft yet focused ear, sniffing out threads to follow, clues to where to go next, prompting the person to flow and sometimes subtly redirecting that flow without being clumsy, obvious or careless. You need to gently allow solutions to present themselves. Be silent, an empty vessel and look for possibilities and hope, accepting that constant change, the interplay of light and dark, yin and yang, is as natural as the beauty that flows in and out of living things. Within darkness there is the seed of light. When helpers have an understanding of a person's beliefs and values, they can treat them with respect, and support change and growth in ways that are consistent with those values.

Values often reflect the 'best' of who we are, often being aspirational. Simply discussing values, bringing them out into the open and putting them where everybody can see them can create real and lasting change. When people discuss their beliefs they quickly become aware of inconsistencies between what they believe and how they behave. This is called a 'cognitive dissonance'. This discrepancy is like a grain of sand in an oyster, a seed that can create a pearl. It irritates and scratches away as the oyster tries to deal with it. Just giving someone the opportunity to discuss their values, out in the open, will often be enough to allow the understanding of any discrepancy to filter through, become an irritant and so create real change. When people realise they have these discrepancies there is a natural and very powerful internal drive to change that behaviour.

You can add momentum and motivation to this process in a gentle way. If you keep a look out for these discrepancies you can open up gentle but motivational discussion around them. Reinforce the value statement, the belief and hope for the future, and then ask what resources or choices they have that will help them to make it come true:

So it is really important to you that your kids have a better life than you. What can you do as a parent that will help them to have a better future?

Well, I suppose I need to make sure that they get to school whether they want to go or not so that they can get a job and earn some money when they leave.

Do not confront people with their behaviour; instead create the opportunity to explore it. Challenging really is counterproductive, the discrepancy may be clear for all to see, but just to make sure reflect the particular point right back at them:

So it is important for you to help your children get a good education.

They have said it, they own the statement and the belief, but to give people time to process this stuff, let it sink in. Allow them to think about it and start to make plans in their own time. Don't push, just relax and observe the flow, watch the confidence and the motivation build.

Connect with their strengths

If you are to be a helper you need to connect with the client's individuality. If you are not able to connect then you and your client are at a real disadvantage; you will not communicate well, you will pull in different directions, you will not dance together, harmonise or find a balance.

If you can help your client to tap into and express their unique skills and abilities, you will do something very important for that person. We all want to be recognised and respected for our uniqueness and our individuality. We all want to feel special, to be independent, to be as much in control of our lives as we are capable of. Just like the rest of us clients want happiness and success but, most of all, they want to feel good about themselves. So an important task as a social worker with a new client is to help people to feel good about the good parts of themselves. To do this you have to find the good parts, you have to find and talk about the client's strengths.

Clients tend to have been told about their weaknesses time and time again, they are often all too aware of them and have been oppressed by them, prevented from growing because of the oft repeated negative messages. Negative messages soon become negative self-talk and then a self-fulfilling prophecy. You can help people to accept they are complicated beings who have both weaknesses and strengths, and help them to accept both sides of their being. Once they have accepted that their way of life is not all wrong, they can begin to explore their strengths and resources. Put things back into balance. They have to learn and accept that they are not wholly bad or good, but their good and bad parts are instead complementary aspects of their wholeness.

Paulo Coelho in 'The Valkyries' talks of exploiting the strong aspects of a person's character to:

> . . . *convince them that they are better people than they had thought . . . when they believed that – their lives changed . . . to work with negative emotions would mean the same thing. He would wind up convincing himself that he was worse than he imagined.*

So talk about things that people are proud of. Ask what they are good at? What resources have they got in the community, socially, environmentally, personally, emotionally and mentally? What have they been good at in the past? What is good about where they live, their son, mother, sister, house, doctor, bus routes, shops, schools, diet, bed, hobbies, pets, environment, people, beliefs, politics, spirituality. The topic itself doesn't matter, what matters is that you give your client the knowledge that they have some strengths. If the client starts to talk about anything in a negative way, try to gently guide them back reminding them that there are plenty of people willing to say negative things about them and we have heard them all before, let's hear about the good stuff. You need to consistently feed these back, using all of your reflective listening and counselling skills:

> *So, you used to be really good at rock climbing?*
> *So it is really helpful to you that the school is just a short bus ride away?*
> *Sometimes your mum helps you when you are finding things difficult.*

When you do this you show that you accept people as balanced human beings with strengths, and so build a good, solid, helping relationship. But far more than this, you are helping them to explore their resources, old, hidden, forgotten, unused or just too familiar. These resources are the things they will use to help them change, they are the building blocks of the future. You are building their confidence in their skills and resources. Helping them feel good about themselves. Looking for resources that will help them cope while they change. Addressing the confidence and motivation equals change equation.

If people say that things don't need to change

Many social workers will recognise the picture of a client who does not communicate about sensitive issues, who act as if those issues or threats are not there, as if nothing is going to happen, as if all is manageable. Clients will say that everything is fine, that they are coping, when clearly everything is not fine. If you think things need to change, you need to identify the path of least resistance and follow it. How do you find and identify the path of least resistance? The answer is that you don't have to, but what you do have to do is let your client find it by looking at their strengths and values and developing a vision of the future.

> *If you want to lead the people, you must learn how to follow them . . .*
> *The best leader follows the will of the people.*
>
> Tao Te Ching

People are often very resistant to change because their whole world and identity is often defined by their behaviour. Change is frightening and they do not know how they will cope. So instead of challenging their behaviour, we ask them what they do want, what is important, what they want for the future, what they want for their children, what they want for their children's future. And so they create a path to explore and become familiar with. We lead by listening. We lead them in a positive direction by inviting them to explore the path. We find the path by asking them what paths they can imagine. We talk about gains rather than losses. What do they want to gain?

Look for open doors

There is a philosophy that focuses a vast amount of attention on resistance and what we can do to overcome it. Taosim is an ancient Eastern philosophy, you have read some quotes from its most famous book, the Tao Te Ching, earlier on. A Taoist would say that they would not humiliate people by challenging beliefs directly. Taoist battle looks for 'win/win' outcomes, so the win they would look for would be empowering and enabling both for themselves and their challenger, neither arguing nor confronting but accepting his challenger's position as a flexible viewpoint liable to change with the correct application of energy.

When they are strong, avoid them.

Tao Te Ching

Motivational Interviewing (MI) is a tool I use constantly with my clients. It focuses on the concept of resistance and is as Taoist as you can get. One of the basic tenets of MI is the concept of rolling with that resistance. In other words, when your client resists your advances, you change your approach. For instance, I often work with clients who misuse drink or drugs and resistance is often identified by the client saying:

It isn't a problem – I can stop anytime

Instead of increasing resistance by confronting it head on and expressing doubts, I change direction and ask:

Is it a problem for somebody else?
I suppose it's a problem for social services, otherwise you wouldn't be here.
Why do you think I would be bothered about it?
Because of the children.
How might it affect the children?
It doesn't affect the children.
Does it affect family life at all?
Not really.
Not really?
No.
Would the children say that?
They might say that they wanted me to stop.
Why?
I suppose they might be worried about my health.

So you can see that instead of pushing on locked doors I am exploring, looking for slightly open ones so that I can get myself invited in. In practice what I always try to do is get alongside my client rather than in front so, instead of brutally trying to push, pull or cajole the client in a particular direction, it becomes a graceful dance. One leads, then the other, until nobody knows who is leading, we are just travelling together. Like the old Victorian table raising game, nobody knows who is lifting the table, the table just rises, which is what the group sitting around it are all aiming for.

Social work done well is poetry, and people do not realise they are being helped. It is essential to understand that you are not working with a static picture, everything is constantly in a state of change. The essence of life is change. Life itself is an expression of a constantly changing, chaotic universe and because change is inevitable, you use that already existing energy not to force things but to gently steer it in a particular direction – mental Judo.

To dream of harmony: the miracle question

If you push and direct people, they will push back and resist movement, in turn their push on you can make you resistant. Energy is burned up by both of you and you end up staying in one place and getting angry with each other. If you try to create a place for them to go, they will not want it because it is your place and not theirs. If people are to change, they need to feel they are doing it by and for themselves. They need to feel their destination is one they have chosen, where they want to go, a place they feel is appropriate for their culture, their beliefs, their age and gender. Without this feeling, the person inducing them to change is just another element of chaos, controlling their lives and something to be accommodated until somehow it goes away.

To help people break out of their traps, you can help them express and think about their dream of the future. The journey of a thousand miles starts beneath your feet. One of my early steps on the road to change is to ask a very special and powerful question of the client. This is known as the Miracle Question and often it unsticks people and gets them back into the flow again. It can create both the essential qualities of confidence and motivation to change.

We know how fresh and original is each man, even the slowest and dullest. If we come to him right, talk him along, and give him his head, and at least say What do you want? . . . Every man will speak his dream.
Ray Bradbury

The Miracle Question is a standard tool of Solution Focused Brief Therapy (SFBT) and Neuro Linguistic Programming (NLP) and is perhaps one of the most powerful tools around. It is used to help people generate descriptions of their dreams and visions for the future. People often know things need to change, but don't know what change looks like or how they will cope with it. Using this question they dare to dream about a better life for themselves and perhaps to remember hopes and aspirations they once had but somewhere along the line gave up on. The question generates a feeling of hope, planning for the future and often a vast number of treatment solutions. Here it is:

> *After we finish talking I will leave and you will carry on doing what you have to do. Later on you will be asleep in bed. And when you are asleep and the house is very quiet, in the middle of the night, imagine that a miracle happens – and the miracle is that the problems you might have or that other people think you have, all the problems you face, are solved . . . but because all this happens when you are asleep, nobody knows that the problems are all solved . . .*
>
> *So when you slowly wake up, what differences will you notice that will make you wonder if something changed and the problem is solved? What is the first thing you notice?'*

On very rare occasions people may respond with something that is unattainable or unrealistic and you will need to agree with them it would be fantastic to have a big house with horses and a Ferrari, or for their mother to still be alive, or their violent partner to have calmed down, come home and love them again . . .

> *It would be lovely if your mother were still alive.*
> *Yes it would.*
> *You loved her?*
> *Yes*
> *She would be very old now.*
> *Yes.*
> *What else would you notice?*

. . . and move on to what is possible, what they would notice when they woke up in the morning that was different. What else? People will start to talk about positive things happening, real practical things. Keep asking,

'What else would you notice?' Your task is to develop those positive things and build hope. People rarely create unattainable fantasies. When people have problems, their main motivation in life is for those problems to go away, they are fixed on them. They feel a bit silly talking about things that couldn't really happen.

This again is a slow and relaxed process. Don't rush ahead. You need to explore in as much detail as possible. Develop the dream by asking questions like: Where are you living? What are you going to do with your time? How do you feel? Where are the children? How are they getting on? What does your home look like? What are you going to wear this morning? What colours are in your main room? What are you eating for breakfast, what about dinner today? Who is there with you? What do you say? What do they say? What are you going to do at the weekend?

The idea is to create as much detail as possible about a particular day. Not a general fantasy but the day after the miracle, a real and particular day. Your client is visualising an ideal and you need to help them to be imaginative and put flesh on those bones, to make the dream as real as possible. This builds hope and creates motivational energy in the client, they very often describe what they would like as a 'normal' family life.

Often this exercise will result in some goals, for instance:

The social worker would leave me alone.
The kids would get up and sort the school things out and I would make them breakfast while they did this.
I would feel calm and happy and not get angry.

Using this question can get you a very clear understanding of what the individual feels the problems are, you can gather plenty of information about the problems but you have collected that information in a way which is solution focused, which does not focus on problems in isolation. It is a small step to then talk about what the individual needs to do first in order for the children to get up for school and what you can do to help them do it.

Using this Miracle Question has a very positive effect. Suggesting this idea to the imagination is an act of creative visualisation. It helps people rehearse for change, perceive barriers to change and become more comfortable with the idea of change. It reduces resistance to change, makes change feel more attainable and so motivation and confidence grows. When the client feels like this, it is time for them to start setting some goals.

Creating a road map

If people are to move somewhere, they need to have a place to move to. If they are to change, they need to know what change looks like and they need to know when they have got there. It is important not to take a step until you have seen the road. Exercises like the miracle question can show a clear destination. You can help your client develop a clear and rounded picture of how they would like life to develop over the coming weeks and months. You can help them to imagine a goal, a goal that is realistic, and a clear plan of how to get there. In other words, a road map.

Without goals we wander around myopically. As an artist I can sit in front of a sheet of paper and decide to draw a street scene. I sit and look and draw and eventually it is completed. Conversely, I can stand in front of a canvas without direction and just paint what comes into my head. Sometimes nothing will come into my head and I will stay there for ages, before waiting for the right action to make itself known I can make a mark and respond to it. There are a couple of schools of painters who work like this. Abstract expressionists just react to the canvas, often painting very large and very colourful abstract pictures with little or no discernable figurative imagery. You may have come across Jackson Pollock and Mark Rothko. The pictures are beautiful and can be very moving and totally desirable. However, they are made without a clear plan, nobody knows what the picture is going to be like. They are a personal exploration of the artists' creativity and subconscious. Abstract Expressionists can work for weeks, months or years on the same picture, working it over and over again until it becomes right, or it can be finished in an hour or so.

Sometimes social workers work like this too, but it is not very efficient, it can be confusing; nobody knows where they are and are unsure of whether the work is finished. Social work is not about exploring the worker's creativity; it is about using that creativity to get to a better place. A clear goal is needed. A vision of the future. The miracle question can really help with this vision, but often does not tell you how to get there, or how far away it is.

So after asking the miracle question, your role is to suggest that together you set some goals so people are clear about what changes they are going to make. Rule number one about a goal is that the client must state what it is, must define it, must want it and see its value, and it must be in their own words. They need to want to get there, not because you want them to or your manager wants them to, but because they want to change for their own reasons. The client needs to choose their own goal.

I always like to write client's goals down. Better still if the client writes them down. This serves a number of purposes; it lets you both know when your journey together is ended, it helps you create a road map together which can be reviewed if the target should at some point become irrelevant and it provides a record that can be looked back on to measure progress.

I like to write goals down in a very simple and clear way that restates why the person wants to make those changes, for instance a goal could say something like:

David says he needs to deal with his depression, so on Tuesday he will make an appointment with the GP so they can talk about how they might be able to help him.

Jane says she wishes the children would go to school so they can get a good education and improve their chances in the future, so she will set the alarm clock for 0700 and get up on Monday to get the children ready for school.

This use of language keys into the client's reality and anchors their plans and beliefs. Using positive solution-focused language, vague plans become clear plans. And with their own motivational pressure of belief to do something about them, they become actions.

Over the years I have realised that clients often set very similar goals. Misery comes in many forms but happiness means similar things to most of us; friends, family, home, freedom from oppression, creativity. People want to deal with behaviour, they want to get the kids to school, have better relationships, deal with debt or substance problems, move house, get a better job. And although it could well be obvious to you what goals people need to set, or what goals they are going to set, you need to hold your counsel. To clients this is new and exciting stuff, the beginning of a new life and is perhaps the most important thing in the world. It is the first step to their better future and they need to feel in control of it.

Road maps and other plans are opportunities for creativity. If, while on the journey, your client notices a diversion and wants to go a prettier, more helpful or easier route, then they should be enabled to go that way.

If, on the way to their destination, they spot a nicer place, they need to be able to settle there without pressure to stick to the original destination. Goals often change as new and unforeseen opportunities arise.

If you become too attached to a particular outcome, if your mind gets fixed on a particular idea, you will lose creativity and fluidity. The known is just history, but the unknown is a crucible full of the potential to give birth to new and exciting possibilities.

If people have trouble setting goals, on my website www.another-way.co.uk there is a set of cards you can download for free. Just hand the goal cards to the client and ask them to circle things on the cards that they would like to change. Then look through them together and prioritise them. Once they start thinking about them the juices start to flow and they very often come up with dozens of goals.

But goals need to be few in number if they are to be achievable. So you help the client to prioritise their goals if they need your help, and choose just a couple to work on right away.

I am often asked, when I teach this stuff to other professionals, what to do if a client suggests goals that are at odds with what the professional feels needs to be done. What if the client is ignoring a big problem, or focussing on irrelevant or impossible things. If you have done the miracle question, if you have done reflective listening and rolled with resistance and looked for strengths, wishes, hopes and dreams you will find that people are well aware of their problems, more aware than you can ever be, and if you give them a chance they will focus on realities and search for solutions. Nobody wants to be miserable, confused, afraid, they want to be happy, and you are giving them some skills to do that.

Sometimes people make plans and are then unable to act upon them. This is an opportunity to discuss what went wrong and what the individual feels they could do differently if something happens to block their progress toward their goal. It may be that the goal was unrealistic and needs to be changed, or the steps toward it were just too big. This gives the client the opportunity to become aware of their own resistance to change and the real barriers that may exist for them, and dealing with these barriers may in themselves become new goals that will allow progress.

Goals need to be achievable and measurable. Sometimes a single goal is too large to deal with in one chunk and needs to be broken down into steps. You can help your client to break goals down into small steps. For instance, if a parent says that part of their miracle is that the children get to school on time, you need to ask them what they need to do to make this happen. You are, in effect, asking them what responsibility they will take for making change happen. Their answer might be that they need to get up in the morning, get an alarm clock, go to bed earlier or do something about their drinking. Some steps or goals are easier to achieve than others, some take longer, some are a moment's work. Others can take a lifetime.

This section, about creating change has, I hope, given you an idea about a particular style of intervention, a relaxed yet focused style where control is attained by letting go and progress comes out of surrender to experience. Using simple, solution focused questions, and goal setting, both motivation and confidence can be increased.

Barefoot social work is born out of calm and repose, a feeling of stillness which gives birth to movement. A feeling that by suspending time, we have all the time in the world. It feels like all you do is talk and listen; there is no aggression, no stress, no feeling of pressure usually associated with social work in this context. It feels still and relaxed because the client is doing *all* of the work, you are just adding focused energy. To do this, you need to be able to remain calm, to focus your attention 100% on the client's needs with no internal dialogue of your own. You need to be a calm, empty vessel ready to be filled up.

The next section of this book is all about you, how you can become the empty vessel that will allow clients to engage in a process of real change.

. . . before you can hope to enter into any measure of success . . . you must learn how to focus your thought-forces by cultivating calm and repose.

James Allen

Chapter 4

Your Self is the Best Tool That You Have

The most therapeutic part of any intervention is the relationship itself. A sculptor needs to keep their tools sharp and, as you are the best tool that you have, you need to keep yourself sharp. And so this section is all about you and about how you can develop the themes that we ended the last section with; finding calm and repose so that you can focus your thought forces, stay sharp, be more in control of your emotions, reduce internal dialogue and become an empty vessel, for your own sake and for the sake of your clients.

You can survive as a front line professional in this demanding work. You can keep your spirit intact and function holistically and authentically, but the responsibility for that is yours. You need to look after your spirit and your emotions. Nobody will do it for you, nobody will even notice or care that you are not coping until it is too late. You have to take responsibility for these things yourself.

The first step is to work with clients in an authentic and holistic way. Allowing them to find their own way forward is clearly better for them, as any positive change is more likely to be sustained, but it is also much less stressful for you. Pressure, on you and from you, is reduced, fear is diminished because understanding is increased and responsibility for change stays firmly where it belongs, with the client. Assessments are very much clearer and lead naturally to clear measurable outcomes.

Existence pain

Pressure from above to assess, help people change and make things safe are not the only sources of deep discomfort for social workers. Earlier on in this book I talked about the importance of work, about how what we do expresses our creativity and individuality. Human beings working in some particular professions immerse themselves in relentless, remorseless and senseless sadness and depression. Working with other people's pain touches and draws upon our own basic humanity. The pain of other human beings affects us deeply emotionally, spiritually and even physically. It affects our experiences of life, our struggle for survival and our road to fulfilment. Just sitting with somebody in deep distress can cause us to absorb some of that pain and carry it ourselves. Feelings and emotions are catching. Eventually a blankness can creep up and you may develop a deep feeling of weariness and dissatisfaction; a dullness of spirit. One day you might realise that you too are depressed, that you have not had a real positive emotion in years. Life has become joyless. Then you wonder why you do it and you just want it to stop.

For many people in all walks of life, work itself is drudgery, damaging, hateful or creates feelings of emptiness. It can stifle creativity, alienate us, cause sickness, depression and anger. If we don't address those feelings we easily enter a depressive cycle that leads to sadness, obsessive repetitive behaviour, addiction, overwork, unsuitable relationships and filling time with meaningless pursuits, trivia, soap operas and immersion in celebrity lifestyles. We are pressured to the point where every one of us has colleagues who are on long term sick leave because of stress. These feelings affect every part of your life, your free time, your family, your friends and community, your body, your home and the emotions you create around you. If you feel like this the world is sending you a very clear message, you are not living an authentic life and something has to change.

When it feels as if there is no balance, as if the scale is all tilted one way, sometimes our response to this imbalance is to try to tilt the scales back. If there is misery on one side, we are inclined to try to add fun to the other side to create a balance. Sometimes this works and makes you feel better for a while, but it is rarely a permanent fix. Eventually you have no energy left for fun, get tired and stop even trying to have fun and end up back where you started.

Adding things to the other side of the scale can end up with you exercising too hard, getting into a smoking/quitting, dieting/binging or drinking/detoxing cycle, watching too much television and feeling more miserable, exhausted and heavy, with an increased feeling of unease. This is not sustainable. To deal with this imbalance permanently you need to address the feelings directly, rather than just try to compensate for them.

Piling stuff up on the scales just adds more stuff to the whole problem. The work life balance doesn't get sorted, it just ends up with darkness, weight and responsibility on both sides of the scale. The solution is to take things off the scale, simplify and add lightness to your life. In other words, if there is anger, tiredness or frustration, then you need to try to reduce these feelings as well as perhaps adding more positive stuff to your life.

In Vedic philosophy there are three conditions of life: becoming, being and decline. Many people are driven to avoid the last two conditions. The western angle on this is to strive to constantly be in a state of 'becoming', in this state we feel we are moving, going somewhere, following a goal. But while it is important to have goals and to strive to develop our individual creativity, that is only part of living a complete and balanced life. If you do not create and maintain balance, you perpetually live in the future and are disconnected from the present reality of your life. This is one of the sources of existence pain. The eternal present moment, and the joys it can bring, pass by unnoticed. You make plans and have dreams but avoid being in your own life from moment to moment, living out of your skin and out of the world around you, your life existing in your head, in the future or the past.

In this state we avoid thoughts of the impermanence of life and the inevitability of death. We reinforce the myth of permanence by having and doing things. If we are constantly in a state of 'becoming' we can make plans, think about changing things, hope that things will get better; we make plans which depend on winning the lottery, not accepting 'what is'. We are always doing something, buying things, developing attachments to things and activities. We convince ourselves that we are perpetually 'becoming', going somewhere, and that our life has some kind of meaning without us ever asking the question or finding a satisfactory answer. Philosophically it is the act of denying our mortality. We create projects, things to do that give us the illusion of being immortal, things that give the impression of a life that is important and permanent. And yet these are the very attachments that give rise to existence pain.

At the opposite side of the wheel is the state of 'being'. This is a state of relaxed living; sharing, communicating or being alone, responding appropriately to the people and environment but not striving, worrying or hanging on to things. Think about those times when you are driving along in your car, not thinking about anything at all, just driving and doing it the best you can, times when you are not being a machine, or times when you are with friends, relaxed, creative and happy, with no agenda, no point to make, no points to score, no sense of being competitive, no planning or thinking what to say next, no fear or concern, just feeling companionable warmth and enjoying the moment. Or walking along the beach, looking out to sea, or watching the trees, the wind or the rain through your window without thought. Playing your guitar, singing in the shower, drawing a picture of your lover, just enjoying the moment. These are states of 'being' rather than 'doing' or 'becoming'. A life out of balance is a life without this state of 'being'. 'Being' is not highly valued in our go faster grab everything society but seen merely as the 'gap' between things.

In many cultures, this state of being, the 'gap' between things, is something to be strived for, a source of health, pleasure and understanding. A joyous place to be. For us in the West, the Industrial Revolution started to eat away at the 'gap'. The focus of life moved from 'quality' to 'quantity'. Not better lives but more lives to serve the machines, not better stuff but more stuff, not better time but more time. Things got faster and capitalists worked out that they could get richer if people and machines worked to their full capacity. Machines do not like 'downtime', they keep working non-stop until they break down. Their owners want them that way. It is part of their design. People, on the other hand, need to stop and rest. Sleep is where you rest your brain and body and allow them to grow, the 'gap' is where you rest your mind and your spirit and allow them to grow. Machines do not grow and do not need rest, just occasional repairs.

Detachment

We are prone to define ourselves in terms of the things we are attached to. Ask the question 'Who are you?' and the answer will often be a list of attachments. We are what we own and the things we do, the things we make precious, the things that make us different from each other: 'I am married . . . I ride a motorbike . . . I am a vegetarian . . . I am a social worker . . . I play the harmonica . . . I write poetry and paint pictures . . .' and so on.

Sometimes we even define ourselves by our limitations, by the things we are not or things we don't like, for instance 'I don't eat meat . . . I don't like football . . . I am shy . . . I am scared of cockroaches . . . I am not very good socially . . . I am rubbish at Maths . . . I can't sing for toffee . . . I am boring' and so on. In this way we become attached to our limitations and by repeating them we work towards making those limitations stronger because (repeat the mantra) **what you focus on gets bigger**.

To have a self in the usual understanding of selfhood is to be attached to people, places, ideas, things, images. These attachments are the source of existence pain, yet they are also the source of much pleasure and fun, excitement and enjoyment.

This is really very important, going into the 'gap' is the core of the Buddhist idea of living in the moment. Note I said living *in* the moment and not *for* the moment; there is a massive difference. When we live *in* the moment we experience what each moment provides us, when we live *for* the moment we invest our energies in behaving as if there are to be no more moments, without care for the future or for consequences.

If you can rise above these attachments and find detachment, or go into the gap, you will experience a contentment that allows you to observe life in this moment. You can take a full and active part in this life, enjoy the fun and yet not be at the mercy of emotions. Detachment takes you beyond pleasure and pain, love and hate, petty partisan allegiances. To be detached is to let go of the things that make you different from others and instead to have a relationship with all things. That feeling when you are having fun with friends with no agenda, or simply staring out to sea. To be detached is to go into the 'gap' and simply be.

A family, a job, a home, children, a relationship, all the 'normal' things of life are things we are attached to, and if you were completely and permanently detached you would not want or have any of these things. Few people, monks and ascetics, choose such a life. But it is a choice. Another choice we have, one more realistic or preferable to most of us, is to understand and experience detachment, to control our attachments and then choose to become attached to things for enjoyment and fun, in the full knowledge that they are impermanent like life, like leaves on a stream.

When you are in control of your attachment, when you can turn it on or off, life becomes multi-layered. You find you can let go of attachments and experience new ones. You can do this because you are more aware that you have the power of choice, and that it is you who chooses the quality of your life. You choose whether or not you will allow things, events and people to play with your emotions.

As a social worker I think it is vitally important to be in control of your attachments. You can, when it is appropriate, become attached to the humanity of your client but detached from their story or history. That means being aware of the history but attaching no personal emotional value to it. Any attraction or aversion colours your perception of reality, and so it is important when working as a helper that you can find that place where you are without thought, ego, attraction or aversion. A social worker is an agent of empowerment for service users, and when you bring your own judgements or values to a service user you severely limit their potential. You unconsciously support their view that things cannot change, you co-operate with their failure-based attitude and collude in their failure to move on. When, as a practitioner, you withhold judgement you are open and ready. You deal with actions and reactions as they occur. Detachment makes it easier to take a stand when you need to because you have a clear perspective on your own involvement.

You cannot afford to dislike the humanity of a client, because you will make judgements and real communication will cease. When you do become detached, your ego and its personal individual and self-oriented values take a back seat and you provide individuals or society with a valuable, person-centred, solution-oriented service.

Remember the scene in the film 'Parenthood', where the children's nativity play falls to pieces? At first dad is concerned, embarrassed, humiliated, and even angry at his child's childishness, but then suddenly he lets go of his ego and starts to enjoy himself and the thrill of the ride. When you can recognise the times when your feelings are irrelevant to the situation, and observe those feelings, it becomes easy and natural to detach yourself from them. Then you can watch the world as if it is a great big soap opera and enjoy everything. This is the essence of detachment, and of choosing the miracle over the grievance. In 'Parenthood', by detaching himself from his emotions the dad lives in the moment instead of worrying and fearing, and so expresses love for his child, enjoyment of the chaos and creativity the world has just given him and discards his anger.

Every decision in life is a choice between a grievance and a miracle.
Deepak Chopra

Detachment is a skill that comes when you realise you don't have to go to war every time someone farts in your direction. (I read that line somewhere and if you know where, let me know and I will credit the writer properly.) Feelings come from the ego and are based on judgements. When we learn to stop judging we can just understand and appreciate. The world is going to do whatever it is going to do, no matter how you feel about it. Your feelings are irrelevant to the world. If you could choose how to feel in a situation, wouldn't it be more helpful to experience something positive and helpful rather than something negative and destructive? Well, you do have a choice about how you feel. If you experience an unpleasant or bad feeling; anger, guilt, fear or sadness, you can stop it and experience another feeling instead. When things get rough you can get all emotional about it and become another part of the problem, or you can hang on and enjoy the ride.

The foundation of the ability to tame your mind is the understanding that you are the creator of your own pleasure and pain, you are your own protector . . . your comfort and discomfort are in your own hands.

James Allen

How to experience detachment

So how do you do it? When you have the knack it is really very easy. The hardest thing is remembering to do it and not getting drawn in to the emotion of a situation, or the reactions of your limited ego. Occasionally ask yourself how you are feeling. Observe your emotions, passing no value judgements on them, just observe them and get used to monitoring your feelings. If you catch yourself feeling something irrelevant or unhelpful, just talk to your awareness as if it is something getting in the way. Say to yourself mentally 'go away now, you are not relevant or useful at the moment, I need to be clear right now'. Direct yourself, gently but firmly, to let go of those unhelpful feelings. If it is already too late and you have been drawn right into the middle of some emotional tornado, you may want to take time out to get your adrenaline levels down, count to ten before you open your mouth, as your mother used to say, and switch off that ego.

. . . circumstances can only affect you insofar as you allow them to do so.

James Allen

What other people do, or do not do, is not your responsibility. You can't control what other people think, say or do, but you can control your reactions to what they say or do. If you get sucked in you will react. Stay detached. Let what they say float over you. If you saw a cloud of toxic gas you could either avoid it or walk right into it waving a stick about. I suggest you think of other people's antagonistic comments or behaviours as a cloud of toxic gas they give off due to some out of control poisonous process going on inside them. It could well come from something bad fermenting inside them, but it could be toxic to you because you are particularly sensitive to it, like some people are allergic to peanuts.

If somebody says something you find annoying or irritating ignore it, as if it has nothing to do with you (because it hasn't). Make the choice to only attach yourself to positive things; joy, happiness, learning, growth, harmless fun. Detach yourself from feeling your own harm, pain and suffering. Once you know they exist there is no point enduring them. Nature gave us the ability to look inside ourselves and to learn.

Unfortunately our true nature gets drowned out by television, the hunt for material possessions, cheap and easy entertainment. Like children we want to be entertained and have our desires satisfied. Stop all that stuff and you will find the strength within.

> *if you believe that outward things have the power to make or mar your life . . . you submit to those outward things . . . [they become] your unconditional master . . . you invest them with a power which they themselves do not possess, and you succumb . . .*
>
> James Allen

When you are detached from your ego and your prejudices, you are able to access a lot of personal strength, strength to help other people who are suffering. That suffering will not affect you personally, although you will still feel concern for them and their pain. When you are completely detached you can empathise with other people and understand their suffering while remaining effective.

Detachment exercise

When you look at something for assessment purposes, or even when you sit with a person and make the conscious distinction between yourself as a social worker and the other as a service user, it is as if you are looking at the reality of the world through a narrow tube, cutting off most of the available information, reducing the light and just seeing what you pointedly focus upon; out of context, out of time, out of place.

Have you ever looked at a tree, a mountain, a flower or a person and seen it in its total wholeness? When you look at a leaf in its wholeness it becomes a miracle, unique from every other, its very existence is poetry, perfect, individual and complete.

Life is fascinating and beautiful, and this poetry is all around us; in the street, the office, the faces of the people we pass by. All you have to do to experience that truth and beauty is to be mindful of it. Here's an exercise that will open up this experience to you. I developed it because generally I am a quiet creature, of isolated dark and cool places, I like forests and mountains, gardens, lakes, rivers, the sea, caves. I feel at home in these places. Safe, content but at the same time excited. Bad places for me are crowds of people and cities. But, of course, I have to go into cities and experience the crowds, so I developed an active meditation that opens the place up for me and allows me to feel safe and feel its wholeness.

I urge you to try this exercise. It sounds so simple when you read it, but if you give it a go you will really begin to understand what I am trying to express in this section. I do this exercise all the time, when I am shopping in town, waiting for my wife and daughter to come out of yet another shoe shop with all the other men outside. It makes the waiting time enjoyable, it centres me and each time I get back to being who and what I really am as a human being. It helps me to remember the magnificence in the ordinary:

1. Find a busy place where there are lots of people. Sit on a bench, lean on a wall, sit in a café and watch the people. Try to clear your mind.

2. Just look at people's outlines, as if you were tracing them or going to draw them with a pencil.

3. Watch their outlines and observe the way they move.

4. Don't think about these things or attach any value to them, just notice them. If thoughts start to creep in, let them pass by without judgement of value or engaging in internal dialogue. As if you were just concentrating on making a drawing of what you see.

5. Just observe.

6. If you find yourself on a train of thought, just get off it and carry on looking, tracing people's outlines as if you were making a drawing or a tracing.

7. Do this for at least five minutes, or as long as you like.

That's it, try it.

You will find your mind becoming much quieter. After your mind has quietened, you will see people in a very different way. They cease to be a mass of humanity and become individual people. They all look funny, human, beautiful, every single one of them. Nobody is a perfect glossy magazine individual, even the ones that are classically beautiful have something a bit silly about them, skinny ankles or dry skin, some are fat, some are thin, big jawlines, fat bellies, long noses. Every single person is odd, different, and in their own human way, beautiful and perfect. This is the human race, with all of its strengths and weaknesses. The magnificence in the ordinary.

This meditation makes me feel relaxed and happy in a situation that used to cause me discomfort. Doing this makes my spirit bigger, my life bigger and more enjoyable, my experience of the world deeper. I can go into the city now and be happy, not just able to cope, but actually enjoy being there, feeling connected and whole.

You can do this act of awareness with anything; a person, an ant, a cheesecake. There are many different ways of looking at the same thing, you can learn a lot just by viewing situations in different ways. When you contemplate a mountain, a crowd, a skyscraper, a ladybird or a grain of sand, the mountain, ladybird, crowd, skyscraper, sand, whatever, doesn't change, you do. It becomes a mirror reflecting your state of mind. You become aware of your anxieties, your drivers and emotions grumbling away in the background. When you expand your thinking in this way you grow, you become more, you go beyond limited preoccupations with yourself, your stuff, your world, your importance, your fears, worries, grievances, problems, prejudices and beliefs, likes and dislikes, all those things that trap you and make you smaller and more isolated, you go beyond the things that hold you back and make you less than you really are.

But this is not all, because something even more remarkable happens. You become aware that there is a level at which you and the other, whatever the other is, are the same. You and the leaf are the same, you and the individuals in the crowd are the same, you and the mountain are the same, you and the river are the same. All expressions of life and the universe, all individual, all unique, all perfect and all connected.

This is called active meditation, or mindfulness, and when you start to do this you change forever. Over time it gets easier and easier. You get to the point where you can almost flick a switch, go into the gap where everything is connected and stop worrying, judging, oppressing. You take control of your internal dialogue and cannot help but appreciate things in a much wider and deeper way. Your perceptions change and ordinary things become extraordinary, more full, still remaining everyday things, but you experience them with more fullness. You are less likely to jump to conclusions and see things in particular habitual ways. You become more creative and are free to approach things differently because you have expanded your mind beyond it's own internal dialogue, worries and concerns, petty ego squabbles and allowed something else to come in without being filtered.

What you experience is the wholeness of life itself and yourself as an integral part of it. Connectedness. You start to realise that many of the things you do, the things you believe in, many of your attitudes, disconnect and make you separate and smaller, less than you really are. And so a process of growing begins. Your compassion grows, your love grows, your hope grows, your humanity gets bigger and deeper, you grow and mature. As a social worker it is a remarkable thing to be able to work with people, allow them to grow and become something else without prejudice interfering with that process.

If you enjoy this experience there are plenty of other ways to attain and use this relaxed aware state. See the resources section at the end of the book.

Connections

For a social worker being able to perceive interconnectedness is a vital skill. When working with families or individuals we need to take a broad view, need to perceive relationships between people and other people, things, feelings, attitudes, places, times, cultural mores and habits. If we are not able to perceive these relationships and systems, key areas will be missed and we will not be aware of the wholeness, only fragments.

Perceiving the wholeness and interconnectedness of life is a key barefoot task. Without that wholeness we are isolated from the flow of information, and when we are isolated we have to rely on our own internal catalogue of ideas to fill in the gaps. This catalogue is full of preconceptions and prejudices and they will prevent us seeing new options and approaches.

When you fill in gaps with your own preconceptions you tend to get stuck in problems and crises and so make faulty decisions and conclusions. Your view of the situation is inaccurate, it has come from inside your head rather than the reality of the situation. This is arrogance and tends to cause yet more problems and make them worse. This leads to frustration, feelings of inadequacy and insecurity. Self-confidence is eroded and it becomes harder to get involved, you become more separate and your doubts about your abilities become self-fulfilling prophecies. You create limits to your abilities and then feel stuck, as if there were no way to move forward.

As human beings develop an ego, a sense of 'I', different from everyone else's, then their sense of connectedness to the world around them becomes obscured, they become separate, isolated in their own bubble. If you are lucky enough to have felt real love, you will know the feeling of selflessness, of being in harmony with another person. Your selfishness and ego fades and suddenly everything about the world becomes beautiful, connected and much more real. You start to feel at one with strangers in the street, stop mentally judging or criticising them and just accept them, with care, as people just like you, trying to get on with their lives.

I like to think that this connected state is the same state that most pack, herd, shoal or flock animals perpetually live in, free from feeling separate, competitive and individualistic. We have all seen shoals of tropical fish on the television, changing direction instantaneously. It happens too fast for each individual member to have picked up a signal or copied another member. There seems to be some level of connectedness. Lyall Watson, in his magnificent book *Supernature* of the 1970s, talked about experiments which showed that individual cells in an organism can communicate instantaneously.

Compassion

The Dalai Lama wrote that developing compassion means holding others back from suffering, and also said that concentrating on the welfare of others will make you happy. Compassion diminishes fright about your own pain, increases inner strength and gives a sense of empowerment and being able to accomplish your own tasks. Compassion makes you invincible.

> *If you can bring happiness and success to another person, happiness and success will be yours.*
>
> Dalai Lama

I have rarely met a compassionate person who couldn't accomplish tasks. The classic symptoms of burnout are the losses of compassion and the ability to complete tasks. Focus turns inward, onto your own pain. The Dalai Lama was emphatic that to become and remain compassionate, the mind has to be tamed. James Allen, an English Christian mystic, wrote extensively in the 1800s about compassion and agreed that you cannot be compassionate if your mind is tainted with internal dialogue, thoughts, value judgements and prejudices:

> *Lose yourself in the welfare of others; forget yourself in all that you do; this is the secret of abounding happiness.*
>
> James Allen

When you let go of yourself you become much more effective as a worker, you do not react from fear or any other emotion, you become at one with the client, spend time in their world, stop trying to be something or do something and actually, because you have stopped trying to be something, you listen and reflect and you become a real help.

> *The Master remains serene in the midst of sorrow . . . because he has given up helping, he is people's greatest help.*
>
> Tao Te Ching

Ram Dass, guru to a generation of Californian hippies, said some damn fine things. He said 'true compassion arises out of the place where I am you'. I think it is one of the most beautiful and poetic of ideas. Of course I cannot become you as an individual. I have to go to the place where we are all the same, let go of my ego and my judgements and my internal dialogue and become an empty vessel. Once I have let go of all the prejudices that are the product of my ego and reach that level where we are all the same, then I can really hear you and find true compassion.

With compassion you work from reality rather than from your own prejudices and can find something positive in any situation. I have often heard social workers say of clients that they can find nothing to like about them, that they have no redeeming qualities, or that working with abusers or violent offenders is difficult. When you let go of your own ego, and your own judgements, this ceases to be a problem and a massive barrier to communication can be overcome. Develop an understanding of this as a person and perhaps together you may find some solutions.

To paraphrase Ram Dass again, 'If you would bring peace to others, then you must relate from that place where you are at peace'. In supervision one day I was in a bad way; stressed, exhausted and full of existential anxiety crap that I had brought to work. My boss reminded me that if I was to be of help to any of my clients I needed to be an empty vessel. Now this is the kind of comment I like from a supervisor. She knows that in order to really communicate and feel compassion, you need to get rid of the 'I' and become one with those around you.

It is paradoxical that the way to become really connected with life and with those around you is to detach yourself. Detachment and connectedness are the same thing. When you detach from your ego, you become connected to the world. Ego isolates you from the world. Your ego is the source of judgement, so when you let go of self you are detached from making judgements and go into a state of being – not doing.

The past and the present

One of the unavoidable products of life is that you create memories of the past. If you look back over your life, you do not see an unbroken linear sequence of events. Some moments and events stand out like pearls in a necklace.

What we focus on in life gets more. What we chose to focus on and remember when we look into the past are jewels that we add to our necklace. In life we can choose to focus on negatives or positives. Good times or bad times, worries and fears or goals and hopes. These are like diamonds and broken glass, mixed up and scattered randomly across the path of our personal journey from birth to death. We can choose to focus on the diamonds and pearls or the rocks and broken glass. We all have both, we all make our choices. Make your choice, rocks or pearls, create your own necklace. Create your own life. Personally I choose to dwell on hope and positivity rather than misery, sadness and failure. My life is a lovely shiny necklace (mostly).

Throughout this book I counsel you to work and live in the present; work with client's present concerns, focus on the here and now, explore peoples dreams and strengths, learn to detach so that you can fully experience the present and not be influenced by the prejudices and values you were given in the past.

If you focus on the moment you can improve on it.

Paulo Coelho

To me some people feel as if they are chased by the past, almost haunted by it, forever looking at what has been, walking backwards into the future, never seeing the present, unaware of the present until it has gone and is a memory. These people seem never to change, are constantly anxious and their concerns remain the same throughout their lives. They have difficulty relating to the future and predicting events, find it hard to accept the unknown or make plans. It is as if they want the future to be as known as the past.

Others seem to have no relationship with the past. As soon as something has gone, their relationship with it ends, as if it never happened. They hop and change from one interest to another, have little stability, leave partners, jobs, careers and interests behind. When they physically move on to another job or home their relationships die. They only look to the future, always making plans and preparing to deal with the unknown.

People focussing excessively on the past or the future will have problems with change, because they do not experience a here and now which is where change happens. With practice, people can destroy the present and only have a past and a future, the present is immeasurably small pieces of moving time that flick by, one after the other, too short to do anything in. By looking backward or forward in time the present gets collapsed. Change happens in the here and now. You must be able to stop the ticking clock and expand the present. By paying attention to the present it expands until eventually, if you get good at it, it expands to fill up the whole of time.

Here's a little exercise to help you expand your present. Spend five minutes each morning just looking without thought. Look through your window at a tree, trace its shape with your eyes as if drawing it. Look at something in your room, maybe a plant, or perhaps something that man and nature have created together, a table. Experience your cat coming to you and wanting to spend time with you. Just watch and listen without thought. Take time to look at a stranger, really look, without adding or removing any value, without internal dialogue and when ideas and thoughts creep in kindly tell them that you are busy right now and let them pass.

Take time to stop every now and then in your day. Park the car for five minutes in a lay-by and be with the trees. Listen to the birds, smell the breeze. Sit at your desk and look out at the seagulls for 60 seconds. Have no thoughts or judgements about these things. Just be. Use your senses instead of your mind.

The past and the future live only in your imagination. The present lives in your senses.

Sorting out your past

People behave in the way they do because of the past. Your past is very closely related to your ability to change. It does not control it, but it can get in the way. Most people have stuff in their past, usually they are aware that this stuff affects them today. They are often told, or feel, that they should 'deal with it'. I was talking with somebody a couple of days ago, using the usual analogy that some of this stuff is 'baggage' meaning you carry it around with you, it is a burden and holds you back and my friend said that she was wrestling with her baggage and had been wrestling with it for some years.

Many well-meaning people would ask what was in the bag, what the baggage was, so that they could get it all out and try to help her to sort it out. But what you pay attention to gets bigger, when you focus your energy on your baggage you give it life and energy, so I asked her if she had ever won this wrestling match, and of course she hadn't because there is always a return bout.

If you were attacked by undefeatable adversaries, like a bunch of tigers, you would not try to wrestle them, you would get the hell out of there and try to put as much distance between you and the tigers as you could. The sensible option, if you have a choice when presented with any kind of fight about the past, is to remain silent and walk away from it. The past is undefeatable, like the tigers. The past happened, it is a fact, fixed solid in time like an old photograph. If you have tried wrestling with it and have never won, then walk away from it or it will eat you up. What you can do is deal with now, how the past affects you now, what you think, feel and do about it.

Dealing with how your past affects you

Make a quick mental list of the people who have wronged you. People you dislike, people whose behaviour offends you. Pick one person and one event out of your list. Anyone, it doesn't matter whether their transgression was big or small. Think about what they did, what hurt or offended you. Then put yourself in their shoes. Did they do it because they wanted to hurt your feelings? Perhaps they were just careless, or had other, more important things on their minds? Maybe they were being selfish? Perhaps they were angry and not in control of themselves? Why do you really think they behaved in this way? Think about it without getting angry, as if you were watching a film and trying to work it out. Be detached.

People do not usually want to hurt your feelings. Your feelings are your own. Unless you try to communicate them, nobody outside knows what they are. If you shout, people may believe you are angry, if you cry they may believe you are sad. But the words angry, sad, happy, calm, convey nothing of the true and complex emotions you may be feeling. If you have ever tried to explain your anger to somebody, you will know how complicated and confusing your feelings really are and how difficult it is to untangle them yourself let alone for others to really understand you. Your feelings only have a life inside your body. Anger, frustration and being offended are poisonous thoughts that harm only you, not only mentally but physically. Why suffer?

The people who offended you are fallible human beings that made a mistake, did something careless, selfish, thoughtless or stupid, driven by their own ego. It is not their job to think about your feelings. You have to look after them yourself. If you often find yourself getting offended or upset then perhaps you need to take control of your feelings. Let them go. Why should you suffer more by running through it over and over? Live your life now, while it is happening. Nothing is happening in the past, there is no change, it is dead and lifeless. Your life is happening now, live it now and make your changes now.

Shadow beliefs

Some of those people in the past may have given you what I call 'shadow beliefs'. These are dark and unhelpful ideas that you now hold about yourself. I like to call them shadow beliefs because a shadow is the absence of light, the absence of intelligence, the absence of illuminating thought. Some of these are the self-limiting thoughts that I referred to in the section on detachment. Negative and unhelpful ideas that you are attached to, that you use to define yourself. Now is the time to throw some light on them.

Below is a list of common beliefs that people have about themselves. Beliefs that prevent them from moving on. Whether they are true or not, they are not helpful, they hinder progress, they prevent change. They are dark and useless.

Circle any of the beliefs that you hold and add any other negative unhelpful beliefs that you have about yourself:

- I am stupid

- I am ugly

- I am weak

- I am wrong

- I am slow

- I am silly

- I am a bad person

- I can never change

- I can never be successful

- I will not be able to survive

- I am too fat

- I am no good

- I am useless

- I am a failure

- I have no taste

- I have no skills

- I have no self control

- I can't help myself

- I am not as good as . . . (who are you not as good as?)

- I

- I

- I

- I

- I

- I

- I

(add your own)

- Pick one of those beliefs.

- Think about who first told you that about yourself?

- How old were you?

- How powerful were they, relative to you, at the time?

- What did that person gain by telling you those things? (Prestige, authority, power, control?)

Now immerse yourself in what has happened since then. Think about your life and events that have contradicted this statement, proved it to be untrue. What are they? What other situations have contradicted this statement?

Do the same for each of your circled shadow beliefs. Search your mind to find contradictory evidence then, on the same page, near the shadow belief, draw a line through the belief, cross it out and write down a statement that contradicts each statement you circled or wrote. For instance, if you chose 'I am stupid', you might want to write something like 'I am clever and creative, I can invent meals, I earned a degree, David thinks I am clever', or 'I am clever, I got good grades at school and I can work out what other people are feeling'. If you chose 'I am ugly', you might want to write something like 'I have had lovers and will have lovers again – the universe is beautiful and I am an expression of that universe'.

Now, I do not know you, I do not know your life, but I am pretty confident when I say that if you really make an effort to look, you will find contradictory statements. One of the characteristics of these self-limiting shadow beliefs is that in one way or another they are all extreme statements. They are cognitive distortions and over generalise, filtering out all the positives and magnifying the negatives. They attach labels and catastrophise. They are all or nothing, with no room for argument, saying 'always' and 'never' and 'I am like this . . .' and 'I am not like that . . .'. The reality is that we all have positives and negatives, none of us is wholly stupid, ugly to everybody we have ever met or failures at everything we have ever tried. And yet, by constantly repeating them internally, we believe them.

Below I want you to write the contradictory beliefs, the statements you used, to challenge your shadow beliefs.

This is really who I am today

_____

_____

_____

_____

_____

My father regularly called me an idiot when I was a child. All through my childhood and early adult life I thought it was true. The proof was that I couldn't do maths and my handwriting was unreadable. So I never tried at school and didn't think I could have any sort of career. I became introverted, shy and withdrawn. Later on I met people who thought I was clever, but didn't believe them, I mistrusted them and thought they said these things to make fun of me or because they didn't really know me and were mistaken or wanted to flatter me for some exploitative reason of their own. I found some excuse to discount their statement. So when people were nice to me, I didn't trust them.

Later still I got fed up with my job as a railway guard and as I loved to draw went back to school. I soon got qualifications, then a degree, in Fine Art. I still thought I was stupid, but lucky. Then, when I got into social work and earned a masters degree, people who were clearly very very clever, doctors, professors and university lecturers, the kind of people I never thought I could be, told me I was clever. They didn't want anything from me, they had no use for me at all, I was just more product to them, output from their institutions. And at last I started to believe perhaps I was not stupid at all. I was forty years old.

Then I learned about the shadow belief technique and understood that a lot of things I thought about myself were untrue. In fact, so much was untrue that I didn't know who I was anymore.

I had always thought I was ugly, slow, dull, stupid and soft. Through using this technique I learned that none of those things were true. They were just things careless people told me which had become part of my world view, reinforced by my internal dialogue. It is vital to challenge your internal dialogue, write your positive statements, read them and believe them.

Here is an important lesson. Children believe everything you say. So be very very careful what you tell them.

Internal dialogue

Unless we practice awareness, wholeness, mindfulness, whatever you want to call it, we rarely observe our inner dialogue with any detachment. Especially our thoughts and beliefs about ourselves and others. We work with a set of beliefs and opinions, many of them put there in childhood, many of them severely flawed. For instance, if you have a habit of saying to yourself 'I could never do that', when you come across some sort of problem such as speaking in public, learning to play an instrument, writing a book or fixing a broken tap, it is pretty certain that you won't be able to do it. Your thought creates the reality. Saying 'I can't' or 'I couldn't' is a self-fulfilling prophecy. You put yourself in a box of your own creation and severely limit your possibilities.

If your internal dialogue, your beliefs and attitudes, thoughts and feelings produce reasons for not taking on new challenges, not taking risks, not exploring what might be possible, not looking at the entirety of the situation and the scope of the problem, then you might be severely limiting your own learning, growth and ability to make changes in your life.

The truth is that you really do not know what you are capable of doing, and if you do not know that, then it is certain you do not know what other people are capable of doing. You do not know what your, or their, true limits really are.

You might surprise yourself if you took on a problem, just for fun and tried something new, something that you were afraid of doing. After leaving school at 16 with no qualifications, I was extremely shy and an undiagnosed dyslexic. I left an abusive home that year, lost my mother, became homeless and lived rough. After working on the railway for six years, I went to art school and became a painter. I have had exhibitions and sold work privately, I have illustrated books and magazines. I became a Buddhist and taught self-hypnosis classes, I have edited a national magazine and run a graphic design business. In the last ten years, since I turned 40, I have been to university again and got an MA, I have written books, learned a musical instrument and spoken in public many times. I did these things for fun, for the challenge, for the sake of taking a risk and expanding my limits, despite being afraid of failure, poverty and of looking stupid, and despite the scars from my past which had convinced me I was unable to do any of these things. But I did them. I was able to do them because I challenged my internal dialogue and for that reason alone.

Wholeness and connectedness are fundamental to our nature as human beings. We all carry scars from our past, they are part of human socialisation. We have all been provided with, and developed and worked, to increase an internal dialogue that keeps us separate, that sets us up as helpless victims in the drama of our lives. You might feel like this, your clients probably do feel like this.

But we were born whole, and we can reconnect and become whole again. We can become as open to the world as little children are, but as adults with experience, compassion and understanding. We do not have to be helpless and when we reconnect through awareness, we go beyond fragmentation and separation and transcend the scarring, the hurt and the fear to rejoin with our fundamental nature of wholeness. These are the gifts you can give to the people you work with. You give them by your compassion, your understanding, your connectedness, your openness, your lack of preconceptions and prejudices.

When you hear your internal dialogue telling you self-limiting thoughts, you must challenge them. Create a new internal dialogue and think: *'that is not who I am any more, you can leave me alone now, I do not need you holding me back any longer'*.

Affirmations

OK, here is a bit of fun. But it does have a serious core. People are very good at telling themselves they are no good at something. We seem to take a national pride in making understatements, being self-effacing and putting ourselves down. If you have negative internal dialogue this exercise can start to put the balance right. We need to get it straight right now that nobody else will ever read this book. Hide it in a really special secret place where nobody will ever think of looking for it. Oh, all right then, put it under your pillow or in the dressing table. This might feel like a bit of hippy nonsense, or something from an American self-help book, but it really does have an amazing effect on how you feel about yourself. The very least it will also do is give you a few moments of amusement. But I guarantee it will do something far more subtle than that.

This might be tricky for some of you, I am going to ask you to think of something nice to say about yourself. Pay yourself a compliment. It could be something like 'Mark, you have got beautiful eyes'. Or 'Mark, you are a wonderful writer', or 'Mark, you have got a wonderful big masculine presence' or 'Mark you are a fantastic harmonica player'. You could go the whole hog and say something like 'Mark you are a very special and unique beautiful expression of the energy of the universe'. (Notice a common theme here?)

Do it like that, with your name at the beginning. Get a pen, or better still a colourful crayon so that it anchors into a childlike part of your brain, and write it down here, nice and big:

OK, now take the book to the bathroom, close and lock the door so you won't be disturbed or embarrassed, look in the mirror, look into your own eyes. With the soft gaze of a lover, read the statement you wrote out loud.

I wrote 'Mark, you are a great big masculine expression of the sexy creativity of the universe'.

When was the last time somebody told you something really nice about yourself? Maybe weeks or months or never, right? But when was the last time you told yourself you were stupid, ugly, fat etc. etc. Yesterday? This morning? How many times this week, this month, this year or in your life have you said stuff like that? You know how self help books and people who like to give advice say you have to learn to love yourself, but never tell you how to do it. Well, this is how you start. Remember, **what you focus on gets bigger**.

So, how did you feel when you did that? Stupid, right, and . . . and a bit happier? A bit more accepting of yourself, perhaps a bit more balanced?

It's a good job my daughter didn't hear me say that, she would have said I was a great big fat blob spewed onto the planet by a chaotic and uncaring universe. But what does she know? The universe may well be chaotic and uncaring – who knows? But that doesn't stop it from being beautiful and creative – and – you pick the necklace you choose to wear. In my world I am a great big masculine expression of the sexy creativity of the universe.

Just to add interest here, I also think that you, yes you, although I don't even know you, I think, no, I know, that you are a wonderful and beautiful expression of the magnificent creativity of this incredible universe. And don't let anybody tell you different.

OK, let's get a bit more serious again and look a little deeper into balance. Firstly with an exercise that I do all the time with the families I work with. This one looks at values, and is based on a set of cards that are free to download from my website.

What's really important to you?

Here's a list of core values. Put yourself in the moment, think about neither the past nor the future. Think about whether each item is an issue in your life right now, and if it is important to you right now draw a circle around it. If it isn't that important right now, just ignore it. Just circle the ones that are important to you today. You might want to think about what each of the statements means to you as an individual and how you achieve that value.

Inner peace	Having a loving family
Doing things I'm supposed to do	Being sober
Being free from drugs	Helping others
Having a good friend	Getting along with other people
Being in control	Living on the edge, taking risks
Being wise	Having power
Accepting things as they are	Being well liked
Having things	Being gentle
Being a leader	Being part of a community
Having a good relationship with God	Having a strong spiritual life
Having lots of money	Living in harmony with others
Being strong	Being the best I can be
Being understanding	Being safe
Being an individual	Being creative
Being really good at something	Being successful
Being in charge of my own life	Being effective
Having things safe and sure	Finding out what makes people tick

Making a contribution	Doing what I'm supposed to do
Being a loving partner	Being a good parent
Sharing with others	Learning and growing
Exploring new ideas	Being whoever I want to be
Excitement and fun	Having lots of interesting things to do
Having enough time	Having free time
Peace and quiet	Being healthy
Having enough money	Having a long and happy relationship
Coming up with bright ideas	Making people laugh
Allowing others to be themselves	Being a good lover
Having beautiful things around me	Being part of a family
Seeing the funny side of things	Being part of a team
Having a close family	Having a comfortable home
Honesty	Having things organised
Having a place I belong	Keeping busy
Managing money well	Having traditions in my life
Fitting in	Thinking about the past
Creating a better future	

If you thought that was difficult, this is where it gets really difficult. Look at all the statements you have circled and choose the six that are most important to you right now. You might have to go back through them and draw stars next to the important ones, maybe even two or three stars next to the really important ones. When you have identified the six most important values to you right now write them here:

1
_____

2
_____

3
_____

4
_____

5
_____

6
_____

You can download a set of value cards from my website that you can use to do this exercise with your clients. People often find this brings them down to earth, to who they are today and to what is important. It is a great exercise to do with families and individuals, because it sets the tone for focusing on the here and now and pays attention to strengths.

Finding the balance between your dark side and your light side

We all have dark and light sides, none of us are 100% crap or totally fantastic. There are good things and bad things about each of us. But at times it can feel as if everything is bad, heavy and without joy. We can easily become out of balance and begin to think of one part of us as more powerful than another. We might pay undue attention to our dark side, start to feel that that is who we are. A balanced life consists of chaos and calm, activity and inactivity. We are all very good at chaos and activity but very few of us are any good at quiet inactivity. But without this we become tired, careworn, and out of balance. The truth is that we are both light and dark, activity and repose and both must be embraced and accepted if we are to feel whole.

Here is an exercise that will help you do that.

Balance meditation

- Take a nice relaxing position, sitting in a chair with both feet on the ground and your hands in a comfortable position on your legs, or lying on your back on the floor. Breathe deeply, into your chest and stomach. Just concentrate on your breathing for a while with your eyes closed.

- Imagine your breath flowing into your hands, your palms, feel how your blood beats, feel how all your attention focuses on your hands.

- Become aware of how the two sides of your body feel.

- Feel how your right hand and your left hand feel.

- Which hand feels brighter, stronger, healthier, more confident, more in control, better?

- Which hand feels darker, confused, lazy, indecisive, weak?

- Give your stronger hand the role of your good hand. This contains all of your potential, your strengths, your ability to find solutions.

- Give your weaker hand your worries, concerns, weaknesses and fears

- The potential is on one side, the problem is on the other.

- Decide which is better and which is worse, the right or the left and all that they symbolise.

- You know both hands belong to you. On the strong side is the ability to solve problems. On the weak side are your problems. Both are part of your life, your situation, your abilities, your humanity. One side is stronger.

- Move your palms together until they meet and clasp. Bring the strong and the weak parts of you together. Take your time and be aware that both hands are part of your wholeness. Everything fits together, a strong bright side and a scared dark side.

The problem and the solution are part of the same wholeness. The solution, the confidence and the power are within you.

Adapted from a meditation by Kay Hoffman.

Don't just do something, sit there! – meditation

Some of the stuff we have been doing in this section of the book are forms of meditation. Meditation is related to the word medicine, it comes from the Latin 'mederi' which means 'to remedy, to right a wrong, to cure, to restore to wholeness'. Mederi itself comes from an earlier Indo-European root meaning 'to measure, to limit, to consider'. Both of these meanings, it appears, apply to the work of the social worker, to measure and assess, and to restore to wholeness.

As social workers we need to meditate upon the wholeness of a service users circumstances, as practitioners we seek to restore to wholeness. Meditation is the practice of becoming an empty vessel, of joining with, and becoming connected to, the world around you, the passive process of being rather than the aggressive process of doing. Being is a state of peace of mind, without expectation or judgement. An empty vessel is full of potential, nothing gets in the way, it can take in what is poured, accepting. Without emptiness there can be no substance poured, no assessment of it, just the assessment of what is in there already. When you become an empty vessel with a client, you start to deal with the reality of their situation not the reality of yours. Peace of mind is not just a journey into your deepest recesses, it is a way of life.

If you find yourself becoming interested in meditation there are lots of classes and books out there to dip into. Meditation takes many forms, including hatha yoga, chanting, whirling like a dervish and staring into candles. It may take you a little while to find a practice that fits in with your beliefs.

When we can let go, we can watch the itch instead of scratching it.

Ram Dass

When you are feeling battered

Sometimes, when we get bogged down in existence pain, we forget who we are. We forget our strengths and forget to do the things we love doing, we can forget the things we are attached to that give us pleasure and instead become totally focused on the things that bring us pain and sadness.

Write a mental list of your favourite creative people; painters, poets, writers, actors, musicians, film directors. Do things that inspire you; listen to music, read poetry, visit the sea or the mountains. Meet and play with friends. A really big part of what you need to do in this life, on this planet, is to be creative, to make poetry out of life, to express your individuality and to enjoy yourself.

You will be working with people who are depressed, anxious, angry, worried and confused. Some of them will be clients, others will be colleagues and managers and some of them may well be your own family! If you are not feeling strong, these powerful emotions will drag you down, kill your spirit and turn you into a pathetic, dowdy TV caricature of a social worker. Newspapers and television will afflict you with more horror. So you need your space, your ability to escape the shod. Your friends and family are an important part of your self-protection system. But even they will fail you sometimes, they have lives and jobs of their own, they can get depressed too and be of no use to you. In fact, they can often be part of your problems, just because you are a social worker. Social workers very often find themselves cast in the role of the 'caring' one in the family, and end up dealing with everybody else's problems as well as their own. This can become a terrible burden, and many find themselves with no clear space in which they can feel safe.

Go for a walk and clear your mind, or do some yoga, go for a run. Clearing your mind allows the creative juices to flow subconsciously. Do something active rather than think or worry about it. You will often find the right answer just comes to you when you are refreshed.

Moods are catching, and you need a system to help you to counteract this. A positive outlook is the first step but that alone will sometimes fail. In this business you get to know many co-workers who are on Prozac, who are exercise junkies or people who self-medicate with too much alcohol, drugs, coffee or tobacco. These things help for a while, they take your mind off the problem, but they store up problems of their own. Such people are easy to spot, look for the stressed-out lives, the suffering partners and children. These people are always late, hot and bothered and full of excuses, yet strangely at the same time they try to take on more, to grab and control. They look for control because life seems so chaotic. These people can be a lot of fun, often very amusing and great with words, but you can't rely on them and will come away feeling massaged by fine words but somehow hollow, tired and drained. Although they give the impression of giving 100%, they are in effect extremely inefficient because they try to do too much and everything ends up suffering.

Leave the herd, be an individual. Find your thing and do it. Express yourself, get creative. Ray Bradbury writes that if you don't get creative, the world will catch up with you and sicken you, the poisons will accumulate and you will begin to die, or act crazy, or both. So paint or learn to play music or dance Flamenco, whatever rocks your boat. If you find it creative, do it or get ill.

Life is a gift and a privilege to be earned. It is not your right to live, it is your goal! Life has given you a gift and, in exchange for the wonderful gift of being, of thought, of animation, asks only that you participate. Different things work for different people. Daytime TV and lifestyle magazines tell us we need 'me time'. Just because this is seen as a cheap, throwaway concept, it isn't any less true. Don't waste your time with psychic vampires, people you know sap your strength and energy, people who will bring you down. There are times when you cannot risk anybody bringing you down, so you need to get time off. Become solitary for a while, meditate, read, walk in the mountains, ride your motorcycle, paint your personal mental landscapes. Play blues on your harmonica. Do things that are just for you and you alone. Read spiritual or inspirational stuff, that remind you of your individuality, your special place in the world. Get back to who you really are.

On the radio today (I love the radio, I would throw away all my televisions today rather than live without a radio) I was listening to some shining light saying that he hated it when people called him a renaissance man, or a jack-of-all-trades. He is known to the public as a writer, sculptor, doctor, comedy actor, musician and television presenter. His argument was that he is curious about his world, exploring, experimenting and simply finding out. And you know what? He was right!

Experiment, look, listen, find out, but do them one at a time. Calmly, peacefully. One thing at a time. Enjoy it, do it well, finish it and move on. Multi-tasking is a myth devised by people who want us to be more like machines, more efficient. If we were good at multi-tasking it would be safe to drive and talk on the 'phone. An Olympic runner never reads a report or does a crossword while they run. They are 100% focused. That is how you get things done properly, safely and completely.

Capitalism thrives on extracting more and more work out of its slaves, and so tries to convince us that we are more efficient if we try to do more. In fact the opposite is true. Happy people are more productive. Relaxed, confident and in control people are the happiest. People who are really good at something make it seem effortless. Do your work then go home. Pay attention, enjoy the experience. You can be good at lots of different things, but not at the same time. You also need to be good at doing nothing. (something I am spectacularly good at to the chagrin of my family!)

Find out what your 'thing' is. Explore and experiment with life, play with it. Take risks, learn an instrument, take up a new and stupid hobby. Write a novel, learn the saxophone, go tap dancing. Yell! Run! Play! Get away from the mud that drags you down! Have fun! Turn off the TV.

A lifelong vegetarian, I recently stopped eating dairy products and became totally vegan. Partly to see what it was like, partly to see how my body reacted, partly because it made sense at the time, partly to lose weight, partly because I cracked open a boiled egg and found a chick in it, partly because I had developed a sinus problem and felt it might help. When people asked me why I had become vegan I gave them a variety of different answers, all true and all depending on how much I felt like talking at the time (I rarely feel like talking). A few weeks later I realised that I could not live without the dirty, sensuous pleasure of a really stinky cheese so I started eating cheese again. The whole vegan thing was an experiment and I learned something. The lesson here is twofold, nothing is as simple as it seems, you must live your life as if nobody was watching and not take it too seriously.

Have fun out of work, but have fun in it too. Think of your heroes, great talents you admire, painters, writers, artists, sculptors, musicians, footballers, scientists, the greatest have a sense of fun in their work. Do you think they were miserable in their work, does misery shine out of it? Nah.

Write a list of stuff you could do if you are feeling battered. I have written a few to get you started:

- Go to my website www.another-way.co.uk and send me an email, a poem, a drawing or a photo of you or your cat. Something that expresses how you feel – I will decorate my office wall with them.

- Write a few filthy words about how bad you feel, spit on it, wipe your backside with it, tear it up and put it in a letter box or the internal mail addressed to yourself so that you can laugh at yourself when you get it back tomorrow, or about five days if your system is anything like ours!

- Go to bed and rest. If you are tired you cannot provide a good service. Social work is often about being strong for people who, at that time, cannot be strong.

- Learn Japanese.

- Dye your hair red or green or blue like you have always secretly wanted to.

- Wear a Hawaiian shirt to work.

- Go to the toyshop and buy a painting by numbers set or a jigsaw or sea monkeys!

- What else have you always wanted to do? Do it!

- Look after your feet; go to the health food shop, buy some peppermint essential oil and some almond oil, put two drops of peppermint oil in your palm and about a teaspoonful of almond oil and take off your shoes, massage your feet with the barefoot peppermint massage oil.

- Paint your toenails – especially if you are a man.

- Learn to play an instrument.

- Go on ebay, buy a knackered van and go to the Big Chill or Glastonbury, maybe I will see you there! (if we can get tickets).

- _____

- _____

- _____

- _____

Celebrate!

You need to take time for yourself to celebrate. To be who you really are. Celebrate your achievements. Every Friday night is a night of celebration in my house. A time to get creative, cook a good meal, put something that feels good on the CD player, stick a few bottles of cava in the fridge, (I can't afford champagne, you would be surprised, (hell no, shocked) at how little dosh you get from writing niche books like this) or even get the cocktail shaker out and make a pina colada. I get into the kitchen, start cooking and think about the good things I have achieved this week, the good things my clients have achieved. Sure, some lousy things might have happened. But good things have usually happened too. It is a flow, a balance, a dance and it all just is.

So take time for yourself because you matter; you matter to your clients, your colleagues, your family and should matter to yourself.

When you are working with clients it's also important that you and they celebrate their achievements. Buy them flowers for God's sake. I have been doing this for years, I have bought clients dozens of cakes and bunches of flowers and only once I had the impression that a client was getting too attached to me. Just once in nine years. That might be just because I am a physically unattractive individual. But all it took to deal with it was honesty. You must be honest from first to last. The most important thing, **ever** in social work is honesty, so be honest, do it, be a human being with your clients, for God's sake, they are people too, so say: 'Hey, you have done really, really well, the kids are happier, things are going great, lets celebrate!' When that one client became too fond of me, I said 'Look, we are getting on really well, we like each other and that's great, because we couldn't do the fantastic things we have done together, you couldn't have worked with me so well and might not have made the great moves you have made if we didn't like each other. But this is my job, it's what I do, I get paid.' And you know, her response was: 'I know, but it is a long time since anybody listened to me or was nice to me, you are a nice man, you care, but I know it's your job and all that, but still, I had to test the water didn't I?'

The moral here, children, is to treat grown-ups like they were grown-ups.

People are not made of cut crystal, they know you are a worker. Worrying about people becoming too dependant is just egocentric and a part of the system that declares workers are in some way different from clients.

In terms of power and income, there are some fundamental differences between us as workers and the clients we support, but our basic humanity, the humanness of the things we do, our motivations, our hopes, wishes and dreams are the same.

The ego is an exquisite instrument. Enjoy it, use it – just don't get lost in it.

Ram Dass

If you have been open and clear, done the things I advocate in this book, you will know when your work is at an end. The end is created as soon as clients set goals. When you have clear goals you will both know what your work is and when it will end. I talk about the end all the way through my work with clients, asking them how they will know that they have got where they want to be, what will be different. Dependence is not a part of this philosophy, it is clear that the client does all the work, makes the moves, takes control. The student who remains a student serves his teacher badly. Make it clear that their role is to take control of their own lives. The end becomes clear and just as the Tao Te Ching advises, you do your work and then leave.

Conclusion

You will have gathered by now that I advocate several things in this book; that you treat clients with respect and that you treat yourself with respect, you remind clients of their strengths and you remember your own strengths, you help clients to understand their motivations and you try to understand your own motivations, you learn to become an empty vessel so that you can approach people without prejudging them, and so that you can escape your own prejudices about yourself, you accept that there is good and bad and that harmony and balance embraces the wholeness of the individual, you feel compassion for others and for yourself, you walk in this world and do the least damage to yourself or others.

Just as an easy reminder I have condensed the ideas into this book into a few thoughts:

1. Be open to your own creativity and the creativity of all other beings. Get creative and respect the creativity of all other beings. Express your individuality, life is too short to be a grey suit (unless you do it in an ironic, postmodernist kind of way!)

2. Have fun, remember who you are and encourage clients to remember who they are.

3. People are usually doing their best with the resources they are aware of. You can help people to have more resources; spiritual, emotional, intellectual, personal. You can share ideas and strategies.

4. Clients have as much to teach you as you have to teach them, often much more.

5. What you pay attention to in life gets bigger.

6. Shut up. Listen ten times more than you speak.

7. Work in the present, the present is a gift, the past has passed (oh, how I struggled to avoid writing that!).

8. Roll with resistance. Do not waste time, energy or peace of mind by banging on locked doors, you will just get bloody knuckles. Look for open doors and welcome mats.

9. Take plenty of time to do absolutely nothing. Learn to totally switch off the internal dialogue and switch on the basic state of connectedness.

It is dangerous to let someone else take responsibility for your choices. It is more dangerous to take responsibility from others, by not allowing free choice!

Ken Saxton, US Barefoot Marathon Runner

I do hope you have found this interesting. I hope you can forgive my occasional rants and that you have found parts of this book useful. If you have, I have included here a list of resources that might help you to take your exploration a bit further.

References and websites

References

Some of these are quoted in this book, others are here just because I think they are worth reading. This is a bit of an eclectic mix, some of which expand on the practicality of the themes I have been looking at.

James Allen (2004) *The Wisdom of James Allen,* Laurel Creek.
  Very thought provoking English mystic.

Insoo Kim Berg and Susan Kelly (2000) *Building Solutions in Child Protective Services.* NY: Norton.

Joanna Blythman (2005) *Shopped, The Shocking Power of British Supermarkets.* London: Fourth Estate.
  You are what you eat.

Ray Bradbury (1992) *Zen in the Art of Writing.* Bantam.

David Brandon (1976) *Zen in the Art of Helping.* Arkana.
  A bit of a curates egg and heavy on the Zen. The author is a social worker and a Buddhist monk. Well worth a read if you can get hold of a copy and quite beautiful in places. Unfortunately out of print.

Deepak Chopra (2003) *Synchro Destiny.* Random House.
  Meditations, from the Guru of the New Age mystical fashionista.

Paulo Coelho (1995) *The Valkyries.* Harper Collins.

Paulo Coelho (1999) *The Alchemist.* Harper Collins.

Adele Coombs (1992) *Barefoot Dreaming.* Albatross Books.

Ram Dass (2002) *One-Liners*. Piatkus Books.

Frank Dattilio and Arthur Freeman (2000) *Cognitive Behavioural Strategies in Crisis Intervention*. Guilford Press.

T.K.V. Desikachar (1999) *The Heart of Yoga*. Inner Traditions International.
  Simply the best book on yoga out there.

Barefoot Doctor (2004) *Manifesto, The Internal Revolution*. Harper Collins.
  How to construct affirmations.

The Dalai Lama (2002) *Advice on Dying: And Living Well by Taming the Mind*. Rider and Co.

Frank Furedi (1988) *Culture of Fear: Risk Taking and the Morality of Low Expectation*. Cassell.

Dennis Greenberger and Christine A. Padesky (1995) *Mind Over Mood, Change How You Feel by Changing the Way You Think*. NY: Guilford Press.
  An excellent cognitive behavioural sourcebook.

John Gribbin (2001) *Stardust: The Cosmic Recycling of Stars, Planets and People*. Penguin.
  You really are made of stars!

Mark Hamer (2005) *Preventing Breakdown*. Lyme Regis: Russell House Publishing.
  Day to day, real world barefoot practice to support and maintain families and prevent children going into care, lots of tools. Read the reviews in this book.

Thomas A Harris (1995) *I'm OK, You're OK*. Arrow Books.

Kay Hoffman (1998) *The Trance Workbook*. Sterling Publishing.

Carl Honore (2005) *In Praise of Slow*. Orion.
  Slow down and chill out.

Jill Kinney, David Haapala and Charlotte Booth (1991) *Keeping Families Together.* NY: Aldine De Gruyter.

Felicity Lawrence (2004) *Not on the Label: What Really Goes Into the Food on Your Plate.* Penguin.
  You will never eat chicken again.

William R Miller and Stephen Rollnick (1991) *Motivational Interviewing: Preparing People to Change Addictive Behaviour.* Guilford Press.

Herbert Otto quoted in Laurence G. Boldt (1999) *Zen and the Art of Making a Living.* Compass Books.

Lou Reed (1996) *Waiting for my Man.* The Velvet Underground and Nico, Polygram Records.

Albert Roberts (Ed.) (1995) *Crisis Intervention and Time Limited Cognitive Treatment.* Sage.

Lao Tzu (2002) (Translated by Stephen Mitchell). *Tao Te Ching: The Book of the Way.* Kyle Cathie.
  Vital, beautiful, poetic, solid – the book of Tao.

Websites

If you visit my website at http://www.another-way.co.uk you will find more ideas and more tools. Some for free, some you can buy.

Food, clothing and lifestyle

http://www. freecycle.org
  My favourite website in the world. Keep usable items out of the landfill by giving away usable stuff that you don't want, de-clutter, reduce consumerism, manufacture fewer goods and meet some nice people.

http://www.howies.co.uk
Very Barefoot, a bit boardsporty. I get some of my organic cotton T-shirts from here and a bunch of my relatives work for them.

http://www.greenfibres.com
Eco friendly skincare, mattresses, bedding and clothing.

http://www.organicfood.co.uk
Ideas about organic food.

http://www.ptree.co.uk
Fairtrade clothing.

http://www.vegsoc.org
About being a vegetarian or . . .

http://www.vegansociety.com
. . . go hardcore – become a vegan! (Ouch!)

http://www.idler.co.uk
I love this site – slowdown!

http://www.barefoot.org
Go barefoot into the world.

Travel and environment

http://www.carbonneutral.com/shop/index.asp
Plant a tree!

http://www.woodlands.co.uk
Buy a woodland.

http://www.foe.co.uk
Become an environmental activist.

http://propertvy org.uk/unique
Buy an unusual place to live.

http://www.bigchill.net
  Go to a chilled out festival . . .

http://www.big-green-gathering.com
  . . . or a big green festival.

Taoism

http://www.taoism.net
  My favourite Taoism site.

http://www.mindmatters.no/tao/rosenthal/introduction.htmlLETGO
  The Tao Te Ching.

Namaste! Mark Hamer, Cardiff, Summer 2006

Preventing Breakdown by Mark Hamer

Offering no-nonsense, evidence-based practice advice. Including a number of practical handouts . . . Rather than a jargon loaded reference book, this 'How to' manual offers simple, effective and tested solutions to crisis situations within families and measurable outcomes for practitioners and families. A comprehensive 'hands-on' resource, it is an invaluable book for practitioners and students.

Community Care, 21–27 April 2005

Should be of interest to any practitioner who works with families in difficulty . . . the tone is intensely practical . . .

Care and Health, 5–11 April 2005

Full of new ideas, this book is a useful guide to developing the family's strengths, developing pride and focussing on solutions . . . an essential book to have at hand.

Childright, April 2005

. . . the work described is inspirational . . . useful ideas about how to work with families . . . the author is passionate about this method . . . a bold title for an inspirational manual . . . I would ask managers to get a copy for the team to share.

Community Practitioner, Vol 78, No 6, June 2005

I feel that this book will be useful to me as a public law practitioner, as a tool in assessing the work that is being undertaken by Local Authorities and residential assessment units. I feel that some of the principles that guide [this] work are crucial to the positive reframing of the work conducted with families whose children are in the care system.

CAFCASS Practice and Research Digest
Jan to April 2005

I will use it in many aspects of . . . my court work when trying to assist local authorities to work with families so that children can be returned to their parents, and I shall refer to it in my writing . . . it is a book that very many people will find immensely helpful.

This is a brilliant book. Every so often I read a book which I really wish I had written: this is one of those. Helping families in distress and adversity to keep together is a huge and vital task: this book explains how to do it. Using the realities of partnership, communication, empowerment, motivation, goal setting, and enabling new skills to be developed, Mark Hamer has provided detailed help to all of us who work in this field. He is to be hugely congratulated.

Professor Richard Velleman, University of Bath and Avon and Wiltshire
Mental health NHS Trust

This . . . reads well . . . it is written from the heart and the passion comes over strongly and is infectious . . . Packed with ideas and exercises, it will inspire practitioners and families. It will be plundered by all staff who wish to find new and creative ways of engaging with families. This book should inspire reflection from policy makers that a primary emphasis on outcomes will also produce good systems and workers with a sense of job satisfaction . . . I could not fault it . . . I could not put it down when I started reading it and that tells you something when I had just spent 7 hours with my children going round a local theme park . . . a gem.

Martin C. Calder, Team Manager, Child protection Unit,
City of Salford Community and Social Services Directorate

The book explains how a front line worker, manager or policy maker can create an environment where families can exploit their potential to develop and protect their children. It offers tools and ideas that will guide workers into building on the family's strengths and self efficacy, developing family pride, a focus on solutions and a determination to succeed.

Social Care Institute for Excellence (SCIE), Social Care Online

Preventing Breakdown: A Manual for Those Working with Families and the Individuals Within Them was published by Russell House Publishing in 2005 (ISBN: 1-903855-61-6). For more information please telephone 01297 443948 or visit www.russellhouse.co.uk